Thrower's Guide to Strength Training

Louie Simmons

THROWER'S GUIDE TO STRENGTH TRAINING

Published by Westside4Athletes®

Made in United States of America.

www.westside-barbell.com

Email: customercare@westside-barbell.com

Cover credit: Charlie Cataline

Copyright ©2019 Westside Barbell

All rights reserved.

ISBN-13: 978-0-9973925-6-2

The Author

Louie Simmons is the founder of the Columbus Ohio Westside Barbell© Club, established in 1986. His members have broken more than 100 all-time world records in powerlifting.

Louie has several decades of special strength training experience for many sports. He has been a consultant for many collegiate and professional teams.

Louie is one of only four men to have made elite totals in five weight classes and was top 10 from 1971 to 2005. He has authored nine books, 15 DVDs, more than 250 articles as well as being a current lecturer. He holds 13 United States patents.

Contents

To the Audience — 1

Chapter 1 Fundamentals of Strength and Power for Throwers — 4

Chapter 2 General Physical Preparation — 13

Chapter 3: Periodization - Division into Training Periods — 17

Chapter 4 The Conjugate System — 88

Chapter 5 Accommodating Resistance — 92

Chapter 6 Explosive Strength through Jumping — 105

Chapter 7 Transition Weight Training from Off Season to Competition Period — 111

Chapter 8 Methods of Strength Training
Part 1-Maximal Effort Method — 116

Chapter 8 Methods of Strength Training
Part 2-Dynamic Method — 121

Chapter 8 Methods of Strength Training
Part 3-Repeated Effort Method — 126

Chapter 9 Combining Weight Training and Throws — 130

References and Selected Bibliography — 153

To the Audience

Although it is my goal to convince both the coach and the athlete that the Westside System can make it possible to combine strength and power training all year long—not just in the off season—by integrating all training efforts together.

This means the athlete must continue to weight train and perform explosive power training during his or her competition period.

It is common to train in blocks for hypertrophy, power, and then strength before the competition period, but then drop all of the blocks with the exception of the events. But, would you do this knowing that a top athlete will lose 10 percent of his or her muscle, power and strength after 14 to 21 days? It can be said that the same holds true as well for technical skills. Unfortunately, many coaches have the thrower weight and power train with no throws, then start a cycle of throws and zero weight training.

The feedback I have received from the throwers I work with show that they realize this does not work optimally. The good news is that all training can coincide to receive the greatest training effects. Many times a weak muscle group can cause a flaw in technical skills—

meaning the throw—and muscle work should not be put aside for long periods of time.

The periodization chapter has many programs to choose from. Most can be done in one hour. This training should be done early in the morning - 7 am or 8 am is best. The throws or sport-specific training should be at 4 pm or 5 pm. All special skills and special strength training can be raised concurrently.

At Westside, the three-week pendulum wave for explosive or speed strength is done year-round no matter the athlete's sports focus. Seventy-two hours later, max effort (M-E) work is done by rotating a special exercise for every workout. Otherwise, when training with 90 percent or above for three weeks, a person will detrain in three weeks.

The Westside System calls for breaking a new record each week. This can be successful at a 95 percent rate indefinitely. Two or three small special exercises are performed after the large barbell exercise. Pick the small special exercise that will increase the lagging muscle group. It could be hamstrings, upper back or shoulders. The rest periods must be kept to a minimum and are dependent on your GPP, which is your level of physical preparedness.

The second workout is separated by six to eight hours for total recovery. Just rest or a special recovery method can be done during the morning and evening workouts.

It makes no sense to lift weights six months during the year, and then throw six months a year. This would give a proficiency of 50 percent. The hardest thing for a human to do is change, but change you must for the betterment of all athletes. It is proven, too, that it is difficult to choose the true potential of seven- to 10-year-olds due to the fact that the strongest boys and girls will dominate the rest. The Westside theory is to insure the strongest boys and girls become the strongest men and women. To become a polished athlete at 19- to 20-years-old, the training must begin in phases starting at 11- through 13-years old.

THROWER'S GUIDE TO STRENGTH TRAINING

Some say there is too much attention to strength. This is a fallacy due to the lack of expert strength training. It makes me think, why can't I be a top college football coach? Maybe coach at Ohio State or Alabama? I don't have any experience. So what? Many high school, college or even pro strength coaches have to prove their knowledge on the platform or make someone extremely strong or powerful.

This is the reason most coaches use machines and no barbells or dumbbells. A machine will build muscle, but not motion. The only coaching degree in America is the Westside Barbell coaching certification and it had a failure rate of 86 percent.

It can take 20 years of doing the wrong training methods before the coach discovers the correct training methods. The point I am trying to make is that too many coaches train their athletes like body builders for looks, while the key to athletic perfection in sports is to teach movements.

Chapter 1
Fundamentals of Strength and Power for Throwers

Let's start by examining the various throws and the strengths needed to be excellent and then move into some basics.

Strength Training for the Shot Put

The technique in shot putting is the same for men and women. Thus, the weight training exercises must be the same. The volume is controlled by your one rep maximum (1 RM) when the emphasis is on bar speed (See Chapter 3, Periodization).

Strength is the most important aspect for the shot putter because it takes great strength to throw long distance. The back must be extremely strong—meaning you must have a strong upper and lower back along with strong legs, hips, trunk and arms. Rotational strength must also be high. The thrower should try to become stronger and faster all the time. Speed also is very important to the shot putter. The athlete must be able to increase force as fast as possible because the shot putter is confined to small 2.13 meter circle. The shot putter must always improve the speed during the release. The release must be 12.5 to 14 meters per second (m/s). This calls for the shot putter to increase maximal strength while becoming faster and more explosive. To do this calls for training all three velocities plus static, overcome by a dynamic movement and jumping.

The Discus Throw

The discus throw is performed with a fast rotation of the body while slinging the implement inside a 2.5 m circle. Like the shot putter, the discus thrower must possess great strength in the legs, trunk and arms, but also must constantly improve their explosive strength. It's simple, the greater the force the thrower can generate against the implement the greater distance of the throw. Speed must be improved as well. Good throwers generate velocity of up to 22 m/s.

Many special exercises must be rotated in training—in other words, using The Conjugate System. The athlete should train for building rotational strength along with a medicine ball, sand bag and a variety of special jumping with and without resistance for both horizontal and vertical jumps.

The Hammer Throw

The hammer thrower is confined to a circle of 2.135 m. He or she must exert force at 27 to 28 m/s to be a top hammer thrower. The athlete must have strong legs, perhaps stronger than for other implements, as well as a strong back and torso muscles.

A good thrower can be gauged by the speed and explosive strength that can be measured by jumping ability. All types of squatting and pulling exercises must be used for strength training. Jumps and short sprints should be used for explosive strength along with med balls, Kettlebells and sand bag throws.

The Javelin Throw

There are no set rules for the run-up to a javelin throw. While the shot, hammer and discus thrower must develop maximal strength, the javelin thrower should concentrate on explosive strength. Explosive strength is the key to throwing farther due to the weight of the javelin. Men throw 800 grams or 1.8 pounds. Women throw a javelin of 600 grams or 1.3 pounds. Because of the force velocity relationship, the weights must be lighter to provide for higher velocity training. Remember, the shot putter's release is close to 14 m/s while the release of a top javelin thrower can be 30 m/s.

Now let's look at the strength training of each sport. The special strength training must address all four phases of a throw.

1. Main phase
2. Wind up phase
3. Preparation phase
4. Recovery phase.

This special weight training must continue all year long. This means including the competition phase. Otherwise, as the season goes along, the thrower's distance starts to decrease. Why? It would decrease because of a reduction of strength and power. A reduction of strength in a single muscle group can lead to shorter distances for the thrower or worst yet development of an injury.

Louie Simmons

Special Wave Periodization

Westside uses a three-week pendulum wave. In a pendulum wave the weight raises each week for three weeks and then rolls back to the first weight. If possible, change the bar on the fourth week when squatting and use a combination of barbell weight and bands for accommodating resistance. The weights for speed strength in the waves would be 50, 55, and 60 percent barbell weight and 25 percent band tension. According to A.D. Ermakov's and N.S. Atanasov's data from 1975 from 780 highly skilled weight lifters, lifters should train at 75, 80, and 85 percent, 50 percent of the time for speed strength. The Chinese use a similar approach for speed strength training. This was based off the snatch and clean and jerk. However, Westside has 85 men having over 800-pound squats that use the same method for speed strength squat training, meaning to maintain roughly 0.8 m/s.

The loading is based off the research of A.S. Prilepin's 1974 data. It shows the optimal number of lifts to be as follows:

- At 70 percent equals 18 lifts
- At 80 percent equals 15 lifts
- At 90 percent equals seven lifts up to a max single.

If your goal is to train speed strength, you must train in the 75 to 85 percent range only. Otherwise, you will be too fast or too slow for the development of speed strength. The thrower must also train for explosive strength; the weight range is 30 to 40 percent for most. Some very strong athletes can use up to 50 percent for explosive strength if velocity is roughly 1 m/s.

For the most explosive strength training, jumping must be employed for highest degree or explosive strength. Explosive strength is the ability to rapidly increase force—the faster the rate of force production, the greater the explosive strength.

THROWER'S GUIDE TO STRENGTH TRAINING

NOTE: Weights should not be measured as light or heavy, but rather fast or slow. This is because special strength is measured in velocities. This is due to the force-velocity relationship: the velocity of movement decreases as the external resistance increases. This also accounts for maximum force (Fmm), which is attained when velocity is small. This information will help you to understand the essence of proper loading for all special strength. You can follow the graph of the three-week pendulum wave system on Page X that shows weights ranging from 200 pounds to 800 pounds. It will work for any lifts, special or classical lifts. It takes time to develop maximal force for a given resistance or motion. This separates the special strengths on the basis of velocity.

1. Explosive strength: Fast velocity
2. Speed strength: Intermediate velocity
3. Strength speed: Slow velocity

Seventy-two hours should separate extreme workouts, which are workouts with high volume or high intensity. After training for explosive or speed strength, the maximal effort method is performed. Where high volume with the barbell is used for the dynamic method, which is lifting non-maximal loads with the highest attainable speed, the maximal effort day is made for working up to a new max on any lift, but mostly special barbell exercises or a special bar each week. To completely avoid accommodation, simply switch to a different special exercise for a one rep max. The athlete should reach the top weight for the day on about the seventh lift. Then call it a day. After the recommended four training days—two for the upper body and two for the lower body—the athlete moves on to small special exercises.

The Westside system calls for training with a barbell 20 percent of the time and 80 percent of the time with small special exercises including jumps. The sequence of training the Westside system uses has two max-effort days for the lower body and upper body on

Monday and Wednesday respectively and dynamic effort days for lower body and upper body on Friday and Saturday respectively. This is very important for full recovery. For most, add one small special workout a week for both upper and lower body. The highest-level athlete can do two small workouts for both the upper and lower.

To be a great thrower, calls for being very strong, especially in the upper back, which includes the traps. Many of the workouts will be pulling exercises from deadlifts to Olympic lifts ranging from snatch and clean and jerk to special pulls for the Olympic lifts. The traps are very important for pushing and pulling. The standard special barbell exercises include squatting, pulling, and pressing, med ball exercises using one arm and then the other, two arm throws from the chest, standing and seated or off the knee (this isolates the arms and shoulders), throwing in the front and overhead, and walking or hopping backwards while pulling a weight sled or while holding Kettlebells.

Body rotation must be constantly improved. Do trunk twists and rotating work with a barbell on your back. Always train the obliques. Push jerk from the back can be an indicator of your shot put. Do 40 special jumps two times a week; see special jumping exercises. Most jumps should have resistance in the form of ankle weights, weighted vest, barbell and Kettlebells while changing the approach from running, seated or after a depth jump—from 12 inches to 30 inches for a high-level athlete—both legs or single leg. Add weight sled pulling for short distances (up to 40 meters) plus normal sprinting. It is easy to track progress in the gym with the barbell and jumps, even short sprinting, but does it carry over to throwing farther?

THROWER'S GUIDE TO STRENGTH TRAINING

NOTE: You must test yourself in and out of the season. Throw from the knees with different weights, off one knee, two knees or seated. Throw with both left and right arm. If your weights in the gym are increasing and your special throws are going further, then your shot, discus, hammer throw or javelin should have greater distance. Standing long jumps or box jumps are a true indicator of your force production. The training for throwers is very similar with the exception of javelin throwing. The javelin thrower must develop mainly the explosive strength due to the lighter weight of the javelin.

While maximum strength is very important to the shot putter, explosive strength is the key indicator to success. The weight coach will oversee the weight and general jump training; but the event coach must train the technique of the thrower. Both coaches plus the thrower must be in harmony. Two methodologies that must co-exist are the conjugate system and the pendulum wave approach to training. While there is a substantial chapter later in the book on periodization, here is a brief explanation of the Westside multiyear three-week wave system.

The wave system is a simple calculation for employing only usable training intensities for explosive or speed strength. It uses mathematics set by Westside as directed from the data of Arosiev for the wave periodization. The loading and volume at certain percentages came from the work of three men: A.D. Ermakov, N.S. Atanasov, and A.S. Prilepin. It came by a controlled group of more than 1,000 high skilled weight lifters and track and field athletes. Intensity is a measure of the percent of a one rep max. The volume is the total weight lifted in a workout. Simply multiply the number of training lifts by the amount of weight lifted.

Periodization is a plan, and without a plan you plan to fail. For throwers, the optimal number of lifts in a workout should be closely monitored. While training in the 70 percent range the total number of lifts is 18, and for the 80 percent range, the total is 15. The three-week waves for speed strength are with weights of 75, 80, and 85 percent. It came be with only barbell weight or a combination of barbell weight and band tension measured at lockout. The barbell weight is 50, 55, and 60 percent and the band tension is 25 percent of a one rep max. The combined method of barbell and bands is superior to all other methods as it adds to an over speed eccentrics phase that causes a virtual effect—meaning a force that is there, but not recognized. There are 50 pages of periodization models to use, but here is one example.

Remember: a new three-week dynamic wave begins on the fourth week!

Week	Exercise	Sets	Reps	Lifts	Percent of 1RM	Accommodating Resistance Percent
1	PUSH-JERK FROM STANDS OVERHEAD	6	3	18	50%	25%
2	PUSH-JERK FROM STANDS OVERHEAD	6	3	18	55%	25%
3	PUSH-JERK FROM STANDS OVERHEAD	5	3	15	60%	25%

Note: "Accommodating Resistance Percent" reflects tension at the top or finish position of the movement!

The second methodology is the conjugate system

Conjugate System

The athlete needs constant stimulation to reach his or her full potential. Stimulation must constantly be changed, or the athlete will succumb to the Law of Accommodation, which says when one uses the same workout over and over, they will have a decrease to their response to training. Therefore, you must change the total work load or volume in a workout.

NOTE: the Westside system changes the total volume in a workout with small special exercises, not the barbell lifts.

THROWER'S GUIDE TO STRENGTH TRAINING

The barbell speed must be monitored closely to verify what special strength is being trained. Not only volume and intensities must change but jumps and special exercises. For example, do calf-ham-glute raises for three weeks then switch to inverse leg curls for three weeks then standard leg curls for the next three weeks.

The theory is simple, everything works, but nothing works forever.

The principle of diminishing returns says that when the program is constantly used over and over, it won't work for the athlete for a long time. Those highest skilled athletes who can compete in two or more Olympics must always change the programming to make further progress. The Westside conjugate system makes it possible to combine general, specific and sport-specific exercises during the entire year.

There can be several reasons highly skilled athletes slow or stop progress. It can be from lack of strength, endurance, explosive strength or even work capacity or mobility or flexibility. The Westside conjugate system makes it possible to interchange or to add work to a single muscle group.

Barbell lifts must be used for training, but one can exchange the barbell for special exercises during the competitive season. This will maintain the basic qualities of the motor system. The conjugate system was necessary to advance the training of high-skill athletes, but Westside starts training young athletes at 14 years old on the very same conjugate system as our world record holders.

The two theories combined together makes it possible to advance the training from the novice to the greatest athlete in the world when one learns to correctly balance general, specific and sports specific exercises throughout all phases of the yearly plan.

Chapter 2
General Physical Preparation

General Physical Preparation (GPP) is the very foundation of the Westside System and can be described as the use of general exercises that are used all year long.

While it is customary to break the year into training blocks with Block Periodization, which leads to a process of detraining by surrendering the work of the previous block, GPP is trained all year long. Progress is measured in the amount of work one can do while maintaining proper technique in your event.

Like Westside, A. P. Bondarchuk, author of *The Olympian Manual for Strength & Size* (2014), found that all special strengths must be increased as well as raising technical skills. All facets of training must blend together or else the training will not bring gains. A multi-year plan must have a hypertrophy, or introductory phase and a power and strength phase while you also master your throwing technique. You must have weight training for Max Effort (M-E), explosive strength and speed strength. You should pay close attention to the Periodization Chapter along with jumping and bounding.

If any part of the above training can be left out of your training schedule, why do it at all? **But, it is important!** Some parts more important than others.

Certain throwers rely heavily on great strength, while others rely on great speed or technique. Strength is more important than speed, for it is your strength that produces speed—F=MA. For those who don't remember Newton's second law of motion, the force (F) acting on an object is equal to the mass (M) of an object times its acceleration (A). Just like jumps, the higher you jump, the more powerful you are.

What is explosive power? Explosive power is the ability to rapidly increase force (Tidow, 1990). The steeper the increase of strength in time the greater the explosive strength. If you gain too much weight or become less strong, your box jumping will decrease along with your explosive power. This is a simple test.

If a thrower does not take care of him or herself, drinks too much, doesn't eat properly, or lacks sleep and is not able to recover, the thrower can suffer due to a lack of physical fitness. Your physical fitness depends on your level of speed, strength, movement, and coordination along with special endurance for fundamental movement abilities.

According to Balsevich and Zaporozhye as well as **Tadeusz Starzynski** and **Thomas Kurz** in their book *Explosive Power and Jumping* (1999), general, specific and sport-specific exercises must be trained together all year long. To do this, simply subtract some special exercises while adding new exercises to the program at different stages of the year. This is the Conjugate System. The Conjugate Training System allows one to add special exercises when needed. If training is interrupted, you fail.

Everything works, but nothing works forever. Or, as the famous Soviet sprint coach Dr. Ben Tabachink said, "To adapt to training is never to fully adapt to training." This is the

THROWER'S GUIDE TO STRENGTH TRAINING

Westside System in its entirety.

The biggest mistake a throw coach can make is to weight train, and then abandon the weight training as you then move on to the outdoor season when you only throw. As your strength suffers from lack of sufficient weight training, you begin the throw season and try to master your technique while some of the muscles that are responsible to maintain your technique are now less than 100 percent. This is a real problem no one has recognized, but never the less is present at all levels of throwing.

A thrower should never run a mile for raising their GPP, nor should they do so-called gassers or weight train like a body builder, meaning lifting medium weights slowly for eight to 12 reps, unless you must gain muscle mass before the season.

A thrower should incorporate short (60 yards) sled walking for the lower or upper body. The M-E weight training must be separated from the fast velocity explosive strength training, but this should only be done when using the Contrast Method. The Contrast Method is defined as lifting 90 percent of a one rep max for one or two reps, then immediately lifting a weight roughly from 30 to 40 percent. Or, exerting against a non moveable bar, then immediately lifting a weight of 30 to 40 percent for a few reps, a workout best done on a Westside trade-marked and patented Static-Dynamic Developer, which is used for weight training, jumping and throwing.

Remember, GPP and SPP should closely resemble each other as not to detrain. Last, but certainly not least, you must use very specific, special exercises along with the GPP to maintain any changes in your posture, your body type or your neuromuscular skills.

For more information, see the following books:

Supertraining, Mel C. Siff, Phd, 2004

Science of Sports Training, Thomas Kurz, 1990

Science and Practice of Strength Training, V. M. Zatsiorsky and W. J. Kraemer, 1995

Strength Manual for Running, Louie Simmons, 2017

Olympic Weightlifting Strength Manual, Louie Simmons, 2016

Special Strength Development for All Sports, Louie Simmons, 2015

Explosive Strength Development for Jumping, Louie Simmons, 2014

Bench Press Manual, Louie Simmons, 2009

Westside Barbell Book of Methods, Louie Simmons, 2007

Squat and Deadlift Manual, Louie Simmons, 2011

It is of the upmost importance to devise a GPP program for a thrower. Cross training with athletes who require much different physical qualities will not bring the desired results. For an example, CrossFit training is great for undirected fitness, but cannot be used for one specific sport, strength or special endurance.

Chapter 3: Periodization - Division into Training Periods

I knew Western periodization was a dead-end as early as 1973, which was the year I broke my back for the first time, but I knew no other way. In 1981 after breaking my L5 the second time, I had to find a better way. I would be strong in one lift, but not the other two. It would be a different lift that would go up while some other lifts were unmanageable. Ricky Crain, a great lifter, would call me with the same story. Dave Waddington, the first 1,000-pound squatter was in my living room and asked how to fix the same problem Ricky and I had. I told him to call me when he found the answer.

So back to 1981, I was desperate. I made a call to Bud Charniga to buy some Soviet books on training. He said, "Lou, you know these are like text books written by their sports scientists on very intricate matters on training." I told Bud that is exactly what I needed because the Western gradual overload system led me down a dead-end road. It is more of a de-training system than anything else. But, enough talking about the past …

Louie Simmons

Three-Week Speed Strength Waves

I looked at the models of Matveyev, his wave system, and the wave-like concentration of loading for five to eight weeks at a time by Verkhoshansky. I then looked at the pendulum approach by Arosiev, which is used for alternating special strength preparation such as speed strength, explosive strength, strength speed and even strength endurance. I also looked at Tudor O. Bompa, Ph.D., and his findings. It was interesting to me how effective the system was that made Naim Suleymanoglu the great Bulgarian weightlifter. I realized the system was for a model athlete or someone of perfect proportion for his sport. It was based on the hypothesis of Felix Meerson (*Plasticeskoe Obezpecenie Organizma*, 1967) and Hiden's findings from 1960 to 1964.

Which one was the best, or was there a best? These were, after all, very intelligent men, to say the least. I had found before that, however, I did not like a long-term plan. I discovered in my training and my training plateaus that after going upward for three weeks, I would regress almost every time. I like the wave system of training by Matveyev and Verkhoshansky, but Vorobyev's (1978) wave plan was a little less restrictive, somewhat like Ermakov's work in 1974.

Dr. Siff asked me how I came up with a three-week speed strength wave. I told him I became no stronger or faster after three weeks, and he was fascinated to hear that because V. Alexez, the great Soviet SHW lifter, used the same three-week wave. On week four, he re-evaluated the training and started a new three-week wave cycle. I think I won Mel Siff over at that point.

There are some different approaches I implement, and I seldom do a regular squat or deadlift. As the meet approaches, we don't reduce special exercises, but push them to the limit to perfect form by concentrating on the weak muscle group. This is what the Conjugate System does. There are three phases that are strength training: Maximal effort, Dynamic Method, and Repetition Method for hypertrophy, which are all trained simultaneously. There is built-in flexibility in a three-week pendulum wave.

Volume and Intensity Zones

The first graphs concerning volume and intensity zones also show the importance of waving the volume and percentage of a one rep max, again to avoid accommodation. The speed strength days show high volume and moderate to low intensity. On max effort days, the opposite will and must occur. The volume is 35 percent to 50 percent of the speed days, but as the intensities must be as high as possible, hopefully, a new all-time record will be set. Like the Bulgarian, the level of preparedness is the major factor for how much one can lift on max effort day.

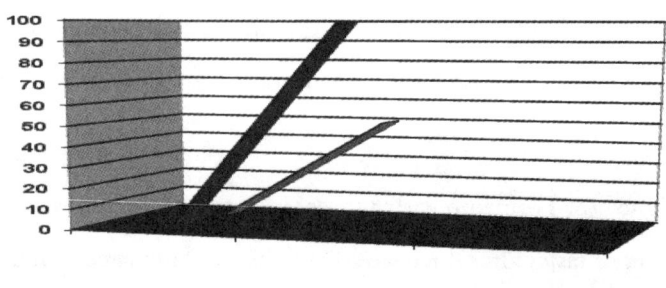

Figure 1.1. Low volume training; highest intensity possible for 100 percent and above. Limit to three lifts of 90 percent and above.

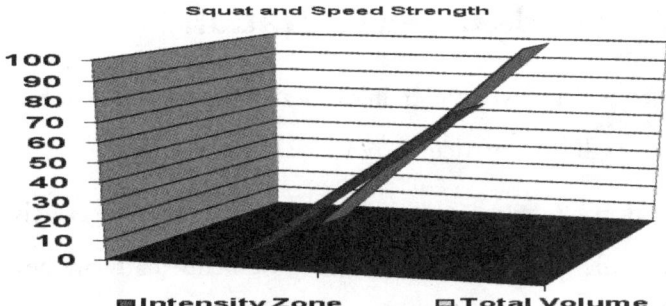

Figure 1.2. High volume training; moderate intensity zones between 60 percent and 85 percent. Limit to 12 to 24 lifts per training session.

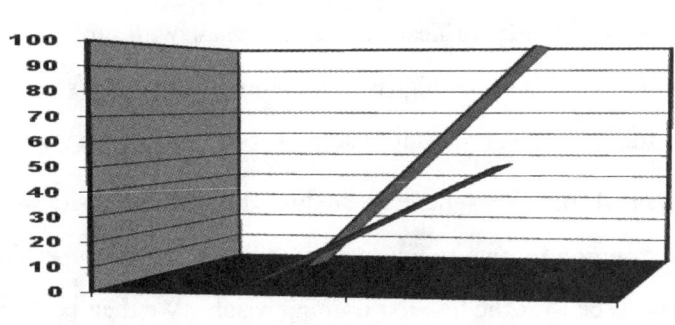

Figure 1.3. High Volume training; low to moderate intensity between 50 percent and 60% percent. Limit 16 to 30 lifts per training session.

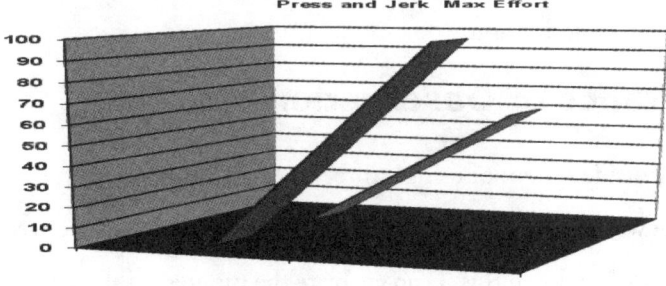

Figure 1.4. Low volume training; highest intensity possible. Limit to three lifts of 90 percent and above.

Four Direct Periods of Periodization

1. **Accumulation** – high volume training of all types to charge or build the body for speed or strength for a particular sport.

2. **Intensification** – now the athlete limits to some degree the exercises concentrating on more specific speed work or strength movements that work best for him or her.

3. **Transformation** – now the value of the previous two cycles is to test while the athlete uses exercises that are most beneficial to the competition. For lifting, the top lifter uses a circa-max or near-max weight phase with limited special exercise that contributes to his or her highest achievements. A runner's work would be very limited to the very most important speed or speed endurance work.

4. **Delayed Transformation** – here, one reduces the high intensity work and relies on rest and restoration for two to four weeks leading up to a competition. We found that 21 days is best for the heaviest training weight. We then taper down to meet time.

It is imperative to know about these phases of training. Refer to the suggested reading for more information on periodization.

The Importance of Observation

During the Westside system of using a three-week wave for speed strength and explosive speed training, the wave rotates from 75 percent to 85 percent in a three-week cycle, jumping five percent per week. By doing this, I can evaluate the progress of the athlete all the time. This makes more sense to observe the athlete to see if he has become stronger or faster as well as other physical qualities such as quickness or where muscle mass should be added.

I don't have a crystal ball, so I have no idea where the athlete's progress will be in 12 weeks or 24 weeks. The three-week wave system allows for better observation on a continuous basis for maximal effort work each week. For maximal effort work each week the major barbell exercises are changed.

Eliminating Accommodation

Soviet sports scientists found after three weeks of weight training at 90 percent or more, progress stopped. This is accommodation, but it is totally eliminated by revolving the barbell exercises each week. We can max out every week throughout the year, and extreme workouts can occur every 72 hours. Our weekly plan is to speed squat on Friday with high volume of 75 percent to 85 percent intensity zone for three reps per set. On Monday it is max effort work for squatting or pulling for max singles. The intensity is 100 percent plus all an individual can do on that particular day similar to the Bulgarian system. No more than three lifts from 90 percent up to a new max. Of course, the volume is low much like the Rule of 60 percent. Speed press and jerks on Sunday. High volume and very low intensity zones range from 40 percent to 50 percent. Wednesday is max effort day, working up to a new personal record or as much as possible. Do this with single lifts not more than three lifts at 90 percent, approaching 100 percent; plus, in one week the speed work is 20 to 30 lifts while the max effort day is three lifts. It is almost a 10 to 1 ratio with speed lifts beginning the 10, and max lifts being 1.

The bulk of our system is special exercises. We do not have a system to form a model athlete, so it may take several combinations of special exercises to make one succeed. Our entire training program is built around special exercises for weight lifting, powerlifting, throwing or running and jumping. I don't concentrate on what you have, but rather what you don't have.

An NFL agent brought in a lineman and asked me what I was going to do. I told him, and he said, "Why aren't you going to run him?" I asked him this question, "He ran for four years and this is how fast he is. Why do you think two more months of running with him will make a difference?" He replied, "Good point."

Nine-Week Training Cycle

Let's look at pendulum waves with special bars. The graphs show a nine-week training cycle, consisting of three different three-week pendulum waves. The nine-week system employs three types of bars. They each have a maximum weight to calculate the percentage. All three maximums are different to avoid the mistake of accommodation or using the same volume repeatedly. The bar path will be somewhat different as well to ensure training all leg and back muscles. The bar speed by percents will be close, but the bar weight is quite different.

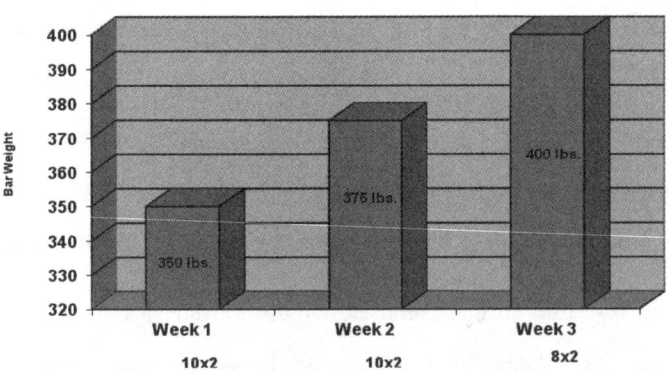

Figure 2.1. This graph shows bar weight for weeks one through three.

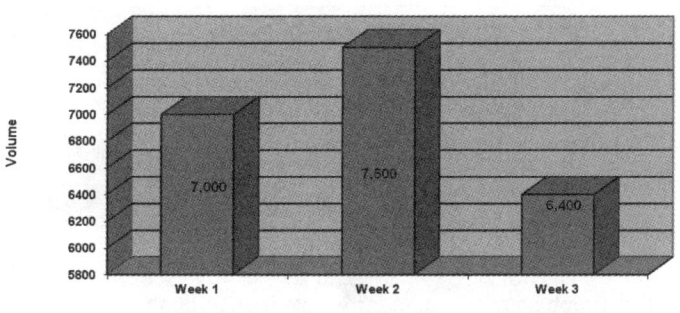

Figure 2.2. This graph shows volume for weeks one through three.

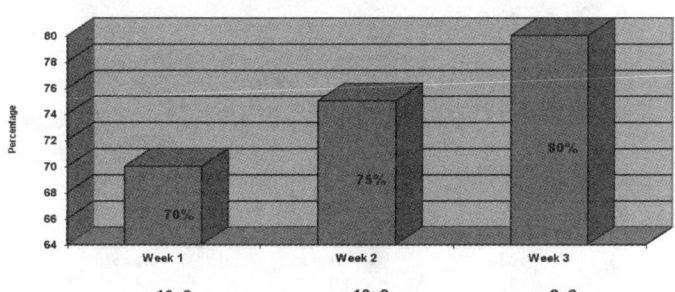

Figure 2.3. This graph shows percentages for weeks one through three.

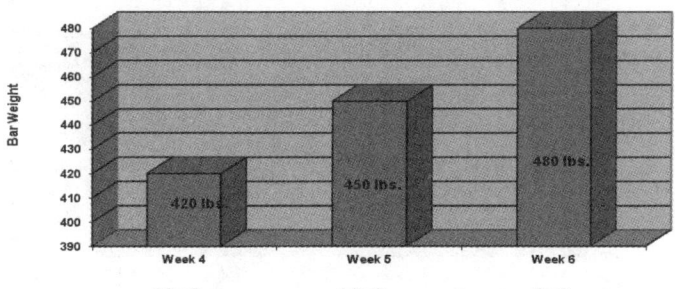

Figure 2.4. This graph shows bar weight for weeks four through six.

THROWER'S GUIDE TO STRENGTH TRAINING

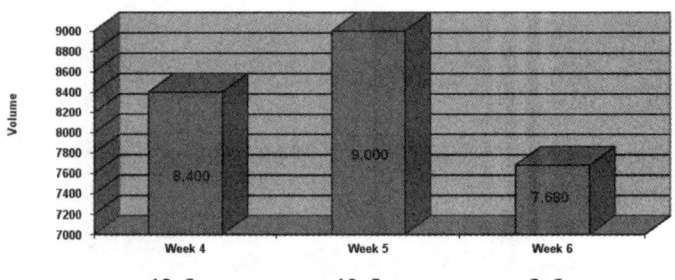

Figure 2.5. This graph shows volume for weeks four through six.

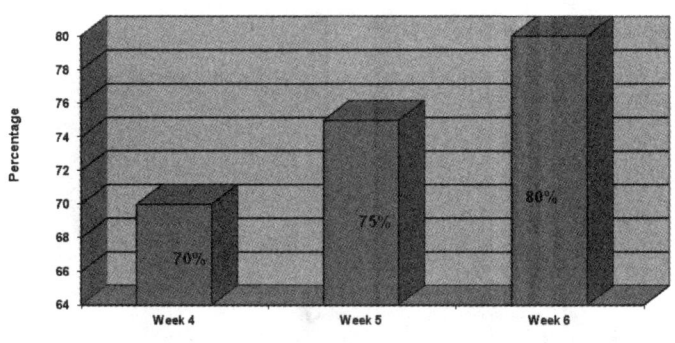

Figure 2.6. This graph shows percentages for weeks four through six.

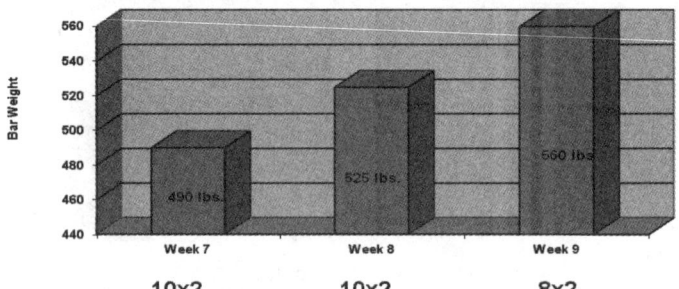

Figure 2.7. This graph shows bar weight for weeks seven through nine.

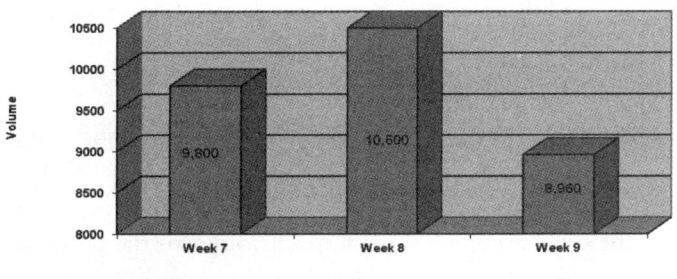

Figure 2.8. This graph shows volume for weeks seven through nine.

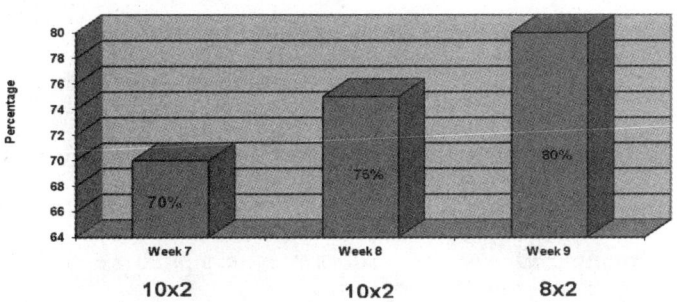

Figure 2.9. This graph shows percentages for weeks seven through nine.

More Wave Cycle Discussion

The wave cycles vary as bands, chains, or combinations of both are added to the barbell to accommodate resistance. When using weight releasers, the added weight on the first eccentric rep phase can be calculated. The variations of a wave are too numerous to list.

The speed strength waves for squatting, jerk, and press normally last three weeks and the strength speed waves last only two weeks due to their severity as well as the near max or circa-max wave phases. If the speed day waves are of ultra-high volume for squatting with speed pulls following, the squats are also of high volume workout.

A speed strength squat day is followed by a maximal effort day 72 hours later; then, a high volume squat and deadlift follows 72 hours afterwards, then they de-load. Most can only sustain three max effort workouts in a row. On deload day, work on special exercises or form.

The next scheduled max effort is replaced by a Repetition Method workout to recover from the severity of such training. Then, embark on as heavy a workload for three or four more workouts. For the squat and pull, this approach works for the pressing days as well, such as standing press or some form of bench pressing flat or angled.

Remember when you feel mentally or physically exhausted, replace the normal speed or max effort workouts with a repetition workout designed for working the less fatigued muscle groups. Repetition work means lots of extensions for the back, hips, arms and trunk.

Note to reader: Speed strength cycles last two or three weeks progressively, going higher in percentage and somewhat higher volume. On max effort days, the barbell exercise must change each week. Example: One week is a squat exercise, a pulling exercise the next, followed by a Goodmorning exercise and occasionally, a repetition day thrown in for recovery for overtaxed muscles. These are in no particular order. Exercises must be chosen for individual goals. Again, repetition work must consist of single joint exercises. Example exercises are back raises, glute/ham raises, tricep extensions, and the like.

Unlike many athletes who have a yearly or even a multi-year plan or the plan and methodology for an Olympic cycle, it is planned with a timetable for developing certain systems. Their concept is to increase intensity while lowering volume, making a functional plan on how fast an individual will be, how high he can jump, or how much he can lift at a particular date during the year. Then and only then will progress be noted. Is the athlete ahead or behind schedule?

Louie Simmons

Monitoring Progress with the Westside System

The Westside system of training can check speed strength every week. This is done with the three-week pendulum wave. Explosive strength can be monitored the same as jumping progress. Maximal strength for upper and lower body is monitored each week. Potential new PRs can be done at over 90 percent sometimes 95 percent year-long. Remember to note the four periods of training—accumulation, intensification, transformation and delayed transformation—are used only in the beginning of training. Then, all aspects are combined simultaneously through a yearly plan.

The Westside system prepares the athlete for the delayed transformation period or the circa-max phase that Westside uses for power meets. It is a wave of the highest intensity; hopefully, a new record of some type is set, depending on the sport. The critical delayed transformation phase or the de-loading phase trains from explosive to maximal strength, covering all elements of strength: coordination, fitness, flexibility, raising lactic acid, aerobic and anaerobic, threshold barriers while increasing V02 max. All components can and must be trained simultaneously. Delayed transformation was adapted from track and field, and Olympic weightlifters from the former Soviet Union.

Periodization can be a weekly, monthly or yearly plan. This plan can lead to a four-year or an Olympic cycle. Speaking of Olympic cycles, a college athlete's sports career can be four years for improving leg and back strength, and there must be a mathematical system to follow. Westside has used the wave system of periodization for more than 30 years with great success. It is, of course, a math problem to be addressed that combines bar speed, total volume and precise intensity zones of a predetermined percent of a one rep max. This along with proper biomechanics and physics can spell certain success. One such plan is outlined next.

The Plan to Move from a 400-Pound to a 1,000-Pound Squat

400-Pound Max Squat

Percent	Weight (pounds)	Reps	Lifts	Band Tension	Volume
50%	200	12x2	24	25%	4,800 lb
55%	220	12x2	24	25%	5,280 lb
60%	240	10x2	20	25%	4,800 lb
Bar Speed is 0.8 m/s avg.					

450-Pound Max Squat

Percent	Weight (pounds)	Reps	Lifts	Band Tension	Volume
50%	225	12x2	24	25%	5,400 lb
55%	250	12x2	24	25%	6,000 lb
60%	270	10x2	20	25%	5,400 lb
Bar Speed is 0.8 m/s avg.					

500-Pound Max Squat

Percent	Weight (pounds)	Reps	Lifts	Band Tension	Volume
50%	250	12x2	24	25%	6,000 lb
55%	275	12x2	24	25%	6,600 lb
60%	300	10x2	20	25%	6,000 lb
Bar Speed is 0.8 m/s avg.					

550-Pound Max Squat

Percent	Weight (pounds)	Reps	Lifts	Band Tension	Volume
50%	275	12x2	24	25%	6,600 lb
55%	300	12x2	24	25%	7,200 lb
60%	330	10x2	20	25%	6,600 lb
Bar Speed is 0.8 m/s avg.					

600-Pound Max Squat

Percent	Weight (pounds)	Reps	Lifts	Band Tension	Volume
50%	300	12x2	24	25%	7,200 lb
55%	330	12x2	24	25%	7,920 lb
60%	360	10x2	20	25%	7,200 lb
Bar Speed is 0.8 m/s avg.					

650-Pound Max Squat

Percent	Weight (pounds)	Reps	Lifts	Band Tension	Volume
50%	325	12x2	24	25%	7,800 lb
55%	355	12x2	24	25%	8,520 lb
60%	390	10x2	20	25%	7,800 lb
Bar Speed is 0.8 m/s avg.					

700-Pound Max Squat

Percent	Weight (pounds)	Reps	Lifts	Band Tension	Volume
50%	350	12x2	24	25%	8,400 lb
55%	385	12x2	24	25%	9,240 lb
60%	420	10x2	20	25%	8,400 lb
Bar Speed is 0.8 m/s avg.					

750-Pound Max Squat

Percent	Weight (pounds)	Reps	Lifts	Band Tension	Volume
50%	375	12x2	24	25%	9,000 lb
55%	425	12x2	24	25%	10,200 lb
60%	450	10x2	20	25%	9,000 lb
Bar Speed is 0.8 m/s avg.					

THROWER'S GUIDE TO STRENGTH TRAINING

800-Pound Max Squat

Percent	Weight (pounds)	Reps	Lifts	Band Tension	Volume
50%	400	12x2	24	25%	9,600 lb
55%	440	12x2	24	25%	10,560 lb
60%	480	10x2	20	25%	9,600 lb
Bar Speed is 0.8 m/s avg.					

850-Pound Max Squat

Percent	Weight (pounds)	Reps	Lifts	Band Tension	Volume
50%	425	12x2	24	25%	10,200 lb
55%	470	12x2	24	25%	11,280 lb
60%	510	10x2	20	25%	10,200 lb
Bar Speed is 0.8 m/s avg.					

900-Pound Max Squat

Percent	Weight (pounds)	Reps	Lifts	Band Tension	Volume
50%	450	12x2	24	25%	10,800 lb
55%	495	12x2	24	25%	11,880 lb
60%	540	10x2	20	25%	10,800 lb
Bar Speed is 0.8 m/s avg.					

950-Pound Max Squat

Percent	Weight (pounds)	Reps	Lifts	Band Tension	Volume
50%	475	12x2	24	25%	11,400 lb
55%	520	12x2	24	25%	12,480 lb
60%	570	10x2	20	25%	11,400 lb
Bar Speed is 0.8 m/s avg.					

1000-Pound Max Squat

Percent	Weight (pounds)	Reps	Lifts	Band Tension	Volume
50%	500	12x2	24	25%	12,000 lb
55%	550	12x2	24	25%	13,200 lb
60%	600	10x2	20	25%	12,000 lb
Bar Speed is 0.8 m/s avg.					

Notice the bar speed is constant, roughly .8 m/s. Notice also that it requires a total of 600 pounds of volume to increase the squat 50 pounds, and the percent range is 50 percent to 60 percent. The rep range and total number of lifts remain the same. The amount of band tension or chains is also constant. The three-week waves for a period of time yields the 50-pound increase by building maximal strength on max effort day, 72 hours later, plus special exercises.

By studying these graphs carefully, it can be seen how mathematics plays a large role in gaining strength and force production.

Let's look at the total volume for a 400-pound max squat. It is one-half of the total volume of an 800-pound max squat. A 400-pound max squat requires one to maintain 4,800 pounds of volume; whereas, 800 pounds involves 9,600 pounds of volume. This is twice as much as a 400-pound squat. A 500-pound squatter must maintain 6,000 pounds of volume. It takes 12,000 pounds to maintain a 1,000-pound squat, which is exactly twice the volume. While the goal as a coach may be to maintain a squat max of 400 pounds or 700 pounds for a lineman to be able to ensure the force development of the before-mentioned squat, the appropriate volume must be adhered to. This is a proven method of strength training, which is referred to as the Dynamic Method.

THROWER'S GUIDE TO STRENGTH TRAINING

The primary goal is to develop a fast rate of force development in sports of all kinds. For those who use a Tendo unit, speed strength is the goal of 0.8 to 0.9 m/s average. Speed strength is trained at intermediate velocities. Know at what velocity a particular special strength is trained or failure will ensue while attempting to improve a special strength. These speeds can be found on page 150 in Mel Siff's *Supertraining*, 2003.

To avoid accommodation in volume in a weekly plan, the special exercises will fluctuate to such an extent that accommodation is impossible. A second method is to change the total volume while training at a certain percent using a three-week wave and a special bar at the same percent. The workload can change.

It is evident that a particular percent—this time 50 percent—can greatly change the work load when doing a back squat compared to a front squat or an overhead squat. The example shows that a typical 500 back squatter would normally have a max front squat of 350 pounds and an overhead squat of an estimated 250 pounds. When looking at the first week wave at 50 percent in the three different squat styles, the total volume per set of two reps would be respectively 500 pounds, 350 pounds, and 250 pounds.

Changing Volume While Maintaining Bar Speed

Max	Percent	Weight (pounds)	Volume
500 lb back squat	50%	250	500 lb per set
350 lb front squat	50%	175	350 lb per set
250 lb overhead squat	50%	125	250 lb per set

This is the simplest way to change volume while maintaining bar speed at the predetermined bar speed at the fixed weekly percent. For more examples, the three graphs below show using chains for a 400-pound max squat; a 600-pound max squat;

and an 800-pound max squat. For benching, the bar weight remains the same, but the accommodating resistance changes accordingly as maximum strength goes up.

Periodization by Percentages

Westside constantly talks about the value of controlling loading by a percentage of a one rep max. This solves the problem of overtraining or detraining. I found the importance of this after applying the advice of A. S. Prilepin's chart for loading at different percentages in *Managing the Training of Weightlifters*. He listed how many repetitions per set as well as how many lifts per workout. His findings show that if the number of lifts are vastly under or over, the training effect decreases. The subject can be thoroughly studied in this book. A sound conclusion was discussed there in A. S. Medvedev's section "A System of Multi-Year Training in Weightlifting."

At the 1964 Olympics, Leonid Zhabotinsky had won the gold medal. Zhabotinsky's volume remained the same for the next two years although his intensity decreased. The result of this was no increase in his total. In 1967, the training intensity was raised and once again the totals started to rise. How does a sportsman increase his lift without overtraining or detraining while maintaining correct bar speed? The answer is a three-week pendulum wave for speed strength development, because it controls volume and intensity for one's strength level.

Below is an outline of a 50-pound jump to raise a squat from 400 pounds to 700 pounds. If strength and speed have not increased by a great deal, the athlete and coach have failed.

THROWER'S GUIDE TO STRENGTH TRAINING

400-Pound Max Squat

Percent	Weight (pounds)	Reps	Lifts	Band Tension	Volume
50%	200	12x2	24	25%	4,800 lb
55%	220	12x2	24	25%	5,280 lb
60%	240	10x2	20	25%	4,800 lb
Bar Speed is 0.8 m/s avg.					

450-Pound Max Squat

Percent	Weight (pounds)	Reps	Lifts	Band Tension	Volume
50%	225	12x2	24	25%	5,400 lb
55%	250	12x2	24	25%	6,000 lb
60%	270	10x2	20	25%	5,400 lb
Bar Speed is 0.8 m/s avg.					

500-Pound Max Squat

Percent	Weight (pounds)	Reps	Lifts	Band Tension	Volume
50%	250	12x2	24	25%	6,000 lb
55%	275	12x2	24	25%	6,600 lb
60%	300	10x2	20	25%	6,000 lb
Bar Speed is 0.8 m/s avg.					

550-Pound Max Squat

Percent	Weight (pounds)	Reps	Lifts	Band Tension	Volume
50%	275	12x2	24	25%	6,600 lb
55%	300	12x2	24	25%	7,200 lb
60%	330	10x2	20	25%	6,600 lb
Bar Speed is 0.8 m/s avg.					

600-Pound Max Squat

Percent	Weight (pounds)	Reps	Lifts	Band Tension	Volume
50%	300	12x2	24	25%	7,200 lb
55%	330	12x2	24	25%	7,920 lb
60%	360	10x2	20	25%	7,200 lb
Bar Speed is 0.8 m/s avg.					

650-Pound Max Squat

Percent	Weight (pounds)	Reps	Lifts	Band Tension	Volume
50%	325	12x2	24	25%	7,800 lb
55%	355	12x2	24	25%	8,520 lb
60%	390	10x2	20	25%	7,800 lb
Bar Speed is 0.8 m/s avg.					

700-Pound Max Squat

Percent	Weight (pounds)	Reps	Lifts	Band Tension	Volume
50%	350	12x2	24	25%	8,400 lb
55%	385	12x2	24	25%	9,240 lb
60%	420	10x2	20	25%	8,400 lb
Bar Speed is 0.8 m/s avg.					

Look at the waves carefully. The bar speed remains the same during each wave regardless of the bar weight. Why is it important regardless if it is 400-pound max as a freshman or a 700-pound max as a senior? Accommodating resistance with bands or chains must be implemented to promote accelerating strength. If strength does not increase, speed won't increase either. To become stronger, volume must increase at the same intensity zones. Each max has a correct amount of volume. Just like the great Olympic champion L. Zhabotinsky found, if volume stays the same, the results will stagnate. This multi-year system perfects skills as strength is increased, and one should be able to use perfect form while using moderate weights. Remember the equation F=ma? Three days or 72 hours later, a max effort day must occur. This builds absolute strength.

Experts such as A.P. Bondarchuk theorize that by perfecting skills, an individual utilizes strength gains. My idea is to increase muscular strength to perfect skills by increasing coordination. I am sure neither Bondarchuk nor I are totally correct, but this system blends both together. This system is simple mathematics.

Look at the rise in strength at 50-pound intervals and the volume climbs 600 pounds at the same intensities. Let's look at the bench press, although any style of pressing can use this system such as overhead presses, push jerks in front or behind the head. The bench waves stay at one constant percent with barbell weight. The change in resistance is made by changing the amount of bands, chains or weight releasers.

Four Examples of a Three-Week Wave

300-pound Max Clean/Snatch

Percentage	Weight (pounds)	Reps	Lifts	Band Tension
50%	150	9x3	27	85 lb
50%	150	9x3	27	85 lb
50%	150	9x3	27	85 lb

300-pound Max Clean/Snatch

Percent	Weight (pounds)	Reps	Lift	Chain Weight
50%	150	9x3	27	80 lb
50%	150	9x3	27	80 lb
50%	150	9x3	27	80 lb

300-pound Max Clean/Snatch

Percent	Weight (pounds)	Reps	Lift	Chain Weight and Band Tension
50%	150	9x3	27	80 lb; 25 lb at top
50%	150	9x3	27	80 lb; 25 lb at top
50%	150	9x3	27	80lb;25 lb at top

300-pound Max Clean/Snatch Lightened Method

Percent	Weight (pounds)	Reps	Lift	Unload Weight
80%	240	9x3	27	60 lb
80%	240	9x3	27	60 lb
80%	240	9x3	27	60 lb

The four examples show that it is the method of accommodating resistance that develops maximal tension throughout the entire range of motion. Many times exercise machines use a special cam with variable lever arms to apply a larger force at the weakest point of the strength curve (V.M. Zatsiorsky). This is done with varying totals of band tension, chain weight or using the lightened method with different amounts of unloading in the bottom. Real weight must be employed. Machines build muscle, not motion. Always use three different grips, none being outside the power lines.

Speed Pulls

Westside uses three types of speed pulls after speed squats:

1. **Speed pulls on floor with bands**

The math is roughly 30 percent band tension at lockout plus 50 percent bar weight of a one rep max. A 700-pound deadlifter would use a 345-pound bar weight plus 220 pounds at top of lift. A three-week wave would look like this:

700-Pound Deadlift

Wide Sumo on Floor				
Week	Weight (pounds)	Reps	Sets	Band Tension
1	345	3	10	220 lb
2	345	8	8	220 lb
3	345	6	6	220 lb

700-Pound Deadlift

Conventional Rack Pulls with Bands				
Week	Weight (pounds)	Reps	Sets	Band Tension
4	345	2	10	250 lb
5	345	2	8	250 lb
6	345	2	6	250 lb

700-Pound Deadlift

Close Sumo on Floor				
Week	Weight (pounds)	Reps	Sets	Band Tension
7	345	1	10	280 lb
8	345	1	8	280 lb
9	345	1	6	280 lb

700-Pound Deadlift

Conventional Rack Pulls				
Week	Weight (pounds)	Reps	Sets	Band Tension
10	315	3	10	350 lb
11	315	3	8	350 lb
12	315	3	6	350 lb

2. **Ultra wide sumo deadlifts with bar weight**

700-Pound Deadlift

Ultra Wide Sumo with Barbell weight			
Week	Weight (pounds)	Reps	Sets
13	500	3	10
14	500	3	8
15	500	3	6

Notice how a three-week wave is constantly altered to avoid accommodation. The weight may vary or the stance may change from sumo to conventional to ultra wide sumo to rack pulls.

3. **Box deadlifts**

Considering box deadlifts, I suggest placing the bar on mats to raise the elevation of the barbell. This maintains the feel of the mechanics of the bar. The band tension also changes each cycle or on the fourth week. The loading graphs are based on a 700-pound max deadlift. All one needs is to do reduce the amount of bar weight and band tension by 50 percent.

350-Pound Deadlift

Conventional Rack Pull with Bands				
Week	Weight (pounds)	Reps	Sets	Band Tension
4	175	2	10	125 lb
5	175	2	8	125 lb
6	175	2	6	125 lb

THROWER'S GUIDE TO STRENGTH TRAINING

350-Pound Deadlift

Close Sumo on Floor				
Week	Weight (pounds)	Reps	Sets	Band Tension
7	175	1	10	140 lb
8	175	1	8	140 lb
9	175	1	6	140 lb

350-Pound Deadlift

Conventional Rack Pull				
Week	Weight (pounds)	Reps	Sets	Band Tension
10	160	3	10	175 lb
11	160	3	8	175 lb
12	160	3	6	175 lb

350-Pound Deadlift

Ultra Wide Sumo with Barbell weight			
Week	Weight (pounds)	Reps	Sets
13	175	3	10
14	175	3	8
15	175	3	6

Again, note that each three-week wave is somehow different. It may be the bar weight, it can be band tension, or it could be altered by a different stance or how far the bar is off of the floor. By using a power rack or by placing plates on rubber mats, one can also stand on a two-inch or four-inch box. A 350-pound deadlift is half or 50 percent of the volume of a 700-pound deadlift. Mathematics is an essential part of weightlifting because a lifter must control the total volume of a training session. The intensity zones or what percent of a one rep max must also be considered. As graphs in this text show, the volume must be highest on speed strength day while the intensities are moderately low to moderate—50 percent to 80 percent. The max effort day would require the intensity zone to possibly be 100 percent plus, allowing the volume to be as low as 35 percent to 50 percent. The loading for power cleans and power snatches without bands or chains must also be regulated.

The training of top weightlifters must use a wide variety of exercises, not just power cleans and power snatches, but the classical clean, jerk and snatch. More than 50 percent of all training must be comprised of special exercises such as back raises, belt squats, inverse curls, box jumps, Reverse Hypers®, Goodmornings, and a wide variety of pulls, squats, jerks and presses.

The Soviets were experts at calculating volume and intensities. Men like A.S. Prilepin, A.D. Ermakov and N.S. Atanasov provided studies in managing and training of weightlifters that determined how many snatch and clean jerks were to be done in a single workout and how many reps, sets, and at what percent these should be monitored.

Although my observations are very close to theirs, I find it is important to train optimally, not maximally or minimally. Plus, we keep percents for weightlifting five percent lower than their recommendations. The data from 1975 by A.D. Ermakov and N.S. Atansov in *Managing and Training of Weightlifters* found roughly 50 percent of the lifts fell between 75 percent and 85 percent. While it is fully recognized this is where speed strength is developed, many lifters today did not grow up doing weight lifting. I propose performing five percent less on each three-week wave.

Example:

300-Pound Power Clean				
Week	Percent	Reps	Sets	Lifts
1	70%	3	6	18
2	75%	3	6	18
3	80%	3	4	12

THROWER'S GUIDE TO STRENGTH TRAINING

This workout can be done after Friday's speed squat workout. You should rest between sets about 90 seconds. This requires good GPP. After all, you are an athlete, right?

250-Pound Power Snatch				
Week	Percent	Reps	Sets	Lifts
1	70%	3	6	18
2	75%	3	6	18
3	80%	3	4	12

This workout can follow a max effort workout on Monday. First, do a max exercise. Example: Low box squats, overhead squat, Goodmornings, box pulls, rack pulls, heavy sled pulls for 60 yards, then rest 90 seconds. You will find that after a heavy lift, a clean or snatch feels lighter and faster. Add variety like band tension of different amounts. I give credit to five great men: Ermakov, Atanasov and Prilepin in *Managing and Training of Weightlifters*, and Verkhoshansky and Medvedev in *A System of Multi-Year Training in Weightlifting*, for not only guiding my career since 1983, but undoubtedly saving my lifting life. I have slightly modified the volume and intensity by using somewhat lighter lifts. One reason is due to a lesser background in GPP and physical preparedness, and second, we use a lot of powerlifting exercises.

A lifter must wave back down after a three-week wave, but also change something else, at least slightly. Vary the amount of bar weight, band tension, chains, weight, box height, pin height, or bars to avoid accommodation. The speed day volume will be the highest while intensity will be at a low 40 percent to moderate 80 percent. Seventy-two hours later on max effort day requires intensity to be a max of that particular day, hopefully meaning a near all-time max or an all-time max on some special exercise. It is gaining strength in the right special exercises that brings forth a next personal best in a clean, in a snatch or in a jerk.

Louie Simmons

If an individual fully understands the process or percents, he will never over train or under train. He needs to alternate weak muscle groups that lead to injuries and constantly make progress until he reaches his sport's potential. Use three, three-week waves before trying a new max. In the beginning, progress is easy, but as an individual starts to lift weights that only a handful of people have ever lifted, it becomes more difficult. It's lonely at the top.

For the weightlifter, it is most important to raise absolute strength to overcome larger loads; to become faster is secondary to strength. This is a common misconception of weightlifting coaches in the United States. After all, world record weights move slower than training weights. An athlete must use the optimal weight for his strength. The amount of work and rest must be monitored as well as movement tempo. Weightlifting requires a great deal of speed and strength. While speed is, of course, a major factor, speed is necessary to lift with strength speed for the development of quick strength.

Weights are 100 percent plus of a max lift. This can be and should be done on max effort workout days. As strength and speed increase at each percent, an individual achieves a new max to work from. This yields a larger training volume. Consider the chart that shows how a 400-max squat volume was 4,800 pounds, and how a 500-max squat would require 6,000 pounds of volume. For every 50 pounds gained in a max squat, a rise in volume of 600 pounds will be factored in at the same 50 percent to 60 percent.

There is much to consider when perfecting form: GPP, recovery methods, relaxation, and above all a selection of the correct special exercises for the individual. Mental, physical, and emotional maturity needs to be considered. Many require a plan. This is a plan for an individual's current strength level and how to raise it correctly. The amount of rest between sets must be a factor because this can be critical for recovery. The percent of a one rep max and the volume the training plan calls for is imperative. This is the Interval Method, much like track athletes use.

With small weights that football players use for speed development, the rest between sets of two reps represents the majority of football plays four to seven seconds. An individual should and must recover in 40 seconds for 12 sets of two reps. For explosive strength development, 24 sets of two reps can be performed with 40 second intervals, which build explosive strength in a fatigue state and represents training at 70 percent to 85 percent. The rest must be 60 seconds to 90 seconds between sets. Max effort work can require two to four minutes rest between singles, which is dependent on the athlete's level of physical preparedness.

The findings of experts like A.S. Prilepin in *Managing and Training of Weightlifters* discovered too many reps per set can change a reduction in force development. It is best to perform high sets and low reps for recovery. The high rep sets should only include special exercises for individual muscles. While his recommendation was with weights at 70 percent to 90 percent, I have concluded that 40 percent to 60 percent provides the same results. If one watches a ball bounce with every preceding bounce, the rebound has less height. Why? It's due to the loss of kinetic energy.

The human body works in a similar fashion with the expenditure of kinetic energy in the soft tissue and muscle fatigue. Repetitions range for explosive strength or explosive power. Starting strength is inherited due to the amount or ratio of fast and slow twitch muscle fiber in the body. The same holds true for absolute strength where one lifts his maximum weight with no time limit. After years of following the guidelines set forth by A.S. Prilepin, A.D. Ermakov, N.S. Atanasov and many other sports experts from the former Soviet Union and along with my own experience over 50 years, I have suggestions for planning sets, reps per workout at a predetermined intensity zone for any athlete after a period of three years of general preparation.

If bar speed is reduced, the set must be stopped because of a power reduction. Pay close attention to the minimal and maximal total reps and amount of lifts per workout. For most, the optimal number of lifts is more beneficial.

Percent	Reps	Lifts
40%	4-8	36
50%	3-6	36
60%	3-6	30
70%	3-6	18
80%	2-4	15
90%	1-2	4-10

If you are greatly above or below the optimal number, the training affects are diminished. These are the recommendations of Louie Simmons, the author.
40% no less than 24 and no more than 48
50% no less than 24 and no more than 48
60% no less than 20 and no more than 40
70% no less than 12 and no more than 24
80% no less than 10 and no more than 20
90% no less than 4 and no more than 10

How to Change Volume at the Same Intensity Zone

Increase your three maxes for a front squat, safety squat bar, and of course, a regular squat bar max. Here is how:

THROWER'S GUIDE TO STRENGTH TRAINING

500-pound Max

Front Squat

Week	Percent	Weight (pounds)	Reps	Lift	Volume
1	50%	250	12x2	24	6,000 lb
2	55%	275	12x2	24	6,600 lb
3	60%	300	10x2	20	6,000 lb
Bar Speed is .8 m/s					

600-pound Max

Safety Squat Bar

Week	Percent	Weight (pounds)	Reps	Lift	Volume
1	50%	300	12x2	24	7,200 lb
2	55%	330	12x2	24	7,920 lb
3	60%	360	10x2	20	7,200 lb
Bar Speed is .8 m/s					

700-pound Max

Regular Squat Bar

Week	Percent	Weight (pounds)	Reps	Lift	Volume
1	50%	350	12x2	24	8,400 lb
2	55%	385	12x2	24	9,240 lb
3	60%	420	10x2	20	8,400 lb
Bar Speed is .8 m/s					

You must pay close attention to these graphs for continued progress in classical barbell lifts including the following: Olympic weightlifting lifts, powerlifting lifts, special squats, Goodmornings, pulls and pressing exercises. Combining mathematics, physics, and biomechanics, your true potential can be reached.

Louie Simmons

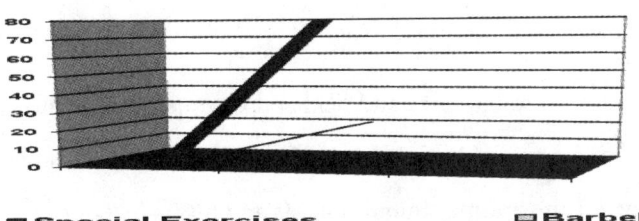

Figure 3: As you can see by this chart, the ratio between barbell and classical lifts is 20 percent barbell exercises and 80 percent special exercises. This is proven by the research done at Westside Barbell by Joe Lasko on powerlifts and Olympic weightlifting as well as track and field. Because athletes are built biomechanically different, it can be dangerous to perform high repetition barbell lifts, as the weakest component of the human can become fatigued and sustain injuries. It is much safer to do special exercises directed to a particular muscle group that may be lacking.

Circa Max

Performed to a Parallel Box

Max Weight	Bar Weight	Weight Percent	Band Tension	Band Percent
800 lb	500 lb	62%	375 lb	47%
850 lb	550 lb	61%	375 lb	44%
900 lb	600 lb	66%	375 lb	42%
950 lb	650 lb	68%	375 lb	39%
1000 lb	600 lb	60%	440 lb	44%
1050 lb	650 lb	62%	440 lb	42%
1100 lb	700 lb	64%	440 lb	40%
1150 lb	750 lb	65%	440 lb	38%

Delayed Transformation Connecting Circa-Max Phase

The data derived in this section is from Ivan Abadzhiev, V. Y. Verkhoshansky, and A.S. Medvedev.

The results at your contest, of course, are of most importance. It requires two proven methods of periodization.

THROWER'S GUIDE TO STRENGTH TRAINING

First, delayed transformation is a period of reducing the amount of volume and reducing the intensity zone somewhat to induce the highest level of sporting skill at contest time.

It was brought about through track and field and Olympic weight lifting from the former Soviet Union. For the squat training, it starts at 35 days out from contest date. Roughly 50 percent sets are done for the optimal amount of sets and lifts. The same is true for 28 days out of your contest.

Now it is interrupted at 21 days, but for Westside, it is a new or all-time record on a box squat. See the circa-max chart above (circa-max meaning near max). A circa-max phase is performed with weights in the range of 90 percent to 97 percent of a one rep max. The number of lifts at those percentages is four minimal, seven optimal and 10 maximal. Westside uses the optimal method, utilizing seven lifts on the circa max day.

An 800-pound squatter after a warm up performs the following:
- 330-pound bar weight x two reps + 375 pounds band tension
- 370-pound bar weight x two reps + 375 pounds band tension
- 420-pound bar weight x one rep + 375 pounds band tension
- 470-pound bar weight x one rep + 375 pounds band tension
- P.R. 510-pound bar weight x one rep + 375 pounds band tension

If an athlete can perform this weight, and if the box height is correct (parallel and good form), he will break a new squat record. During the second week of circa-max, the lifter will work up to approximately 370 pounds for a single.

This concludes the circa-max phase. It represents 21 days out and 14 days out. Now more recovery time is needed. Seven days out large men (275 pounds and up) will not squat, but do only special exercises. Two hundred and forty-two pound men and lighter can squat light. For example: 330 pounds x 2 x 2 with no band tension or if you like 140 pounds of band tension.

As you see, Westside divides the delayed transformation phase in two parts: with extreme stimulus at 21 days out, then back to the delayed transformation through 14 days out to assure all three lifts are at their max on contest day. (Refer to chart x on page x for an explanation of our combination method training by using bands on and bar weight.) This chart is the combined efforts of 75 men who have officially squatted from 800 pounds up to 1,205 pounds. Look carefully at the bar weight percentage and the band tension percentage.

As a lifter progresses from 800 pounds to 950 pounds, the bar percentage goes from 62 percent to 68 percent, causing the band tension to go from 47 percent to 39 percent. This means the bar percent goes up six percent while the band tension goes down eight percent. Let it be noted as well that at 1,000 pounds to 1,150 pounds, the bar percent goes up five percent while the band tension goes down six percent.

I am asked about scientific studies and I can tell you that no one besides Westside has such a study with world class strength athletes. Ours is a work of more than twenty years of experiments. More can be learned about the Delayed Transformation Phase on pg. 30 in *Science and Practice of Strength Training* (Zatsiorsky Circa Max Method 1995; Yerkhoshansky, *Supertraining*, 2009).

Workouts

1. Clean pull, followed by squat clean
2. Jerk barbell taken from stands
3. Clean and jerk starting with barbell below knees
4. Push jerk followed by jerk, barbell taken from stands
5. Clean pull with four stops upwards
6. Power clean, squat, then jerk
7. Clean and jerk starting with barbell at knee level
8. Clean pull from the floor
9. Jerk from behind the head
10. Clean and jerk starting with barbell below the knees
11. Push jerk with barbell taken from stands
12. Clean pull with a medium hand spacing
13. Squat followed by jerk behind the head
14. Classic clean and jerk from the floor
15. 1Power clean starting with barbell at knee level
16. Clean pull standing on a block
17. Push jerk from behind the head followed by overhead squat
18. Front squat followed by jerk
19. Clean pull starting with the barbell at knee level
20. Power clean from the floor
21. Half jerk followed by the jerk with barbell taken from stands
22. Clean pull slowly up plus lower slowly
23. Push jerk after power clean
24. Power clean, push jerk, then overhead squat
25. Clean pull to knee level

Louie Simmons

Pressing for Throwers

To throw world class distances, the athlete must possess a strong upper body. It has to be developed by all types of pressing.

All four angles must be trained—flat, incline, decline seated and standing. The standing would include push press or push jerk from the chest or the back. The push jerk from the back is a good indicator of your progress for the shot. There are testers, meaning a series of special exercises, for the evaluation of your throwing distance. Other special exercises will build the testers. You must find the difference. It does no good to be strong in the wrong exercises.

You must raise your work capacity constantly. Using dumbbells is one way to do this. The former East Germans would do four sets of dumbbells every other day. They are alternated every other day. The dumbbells should be of average weight to make it possible to do four sets of 15 to 20 reps with ease. Each workout uses a different angle. Doing it this way builds all pressing muscles in all directions and safeguards the athlete from injury as well as raising work capacity. This means on some lower body workouts you will be doing upper body pressing. If you do the dumbbells first on both upper and lower body workouts, it functions as a good warmup.

Their pressing volume was optimal: 18 lifts at 70 percent, 15 lifts at 80 percent; and when going into the 90 percent range, up to a new all-time record, the number of lifts to break an all-time record or M-E Method, seven lifts is optimal. This is according to the 1974 data of A. S. Prilepin, the national weight lifting coach of the former Soviet Union.

A sample three-week wave would look like the example below.

400 Max			
Percent	Reps	Sets	Lifts
75%	3	6	18
80%	3	6	18
85%	3	5	15

Westside highly recommends doing ballistic pressing for great reversal strength. Westside also recommends using the Combination of Resistance Method using barbell weight and bands with tension. The method allows the athlete to have the correct amount of weight or resistance at the bottom of the lift as well as the lockout, which is impossible with just weights or with just bands. An added advantage is that the rubber bands will cause an over speed eccentric phase. The combination will build great reversible strength—faster down, faster up.

To test this theory, drop a basketball from a set distance and record its rebound. Next, throw the basketball down with great force. Now record its rebound height. By throwing the ball down with force it will provide great induced deformation through muscle and tendon elasticity.

Ballistic style pressing is lowering—almost dropping—the barbell or dumbbells and immediately stopping the eccentric phase without hitting your body and then pressing concentrically as powerfully as possible. The kinetic energy of the weights falling will be transformed into the body during the amortization phase. The transfer is not fast enough to be plyometric, but rather it is a ballistic action that also relays elastic energy that contributes to the concentric action.

All types of pressing can be ballistic—flat, incline, decline and seated as well as standing. Dumbbells can be done ballistically as well. The amortization phase with dumbbells can be faster than catching medicine balls and releasing them.

Louie Simmons

Special note: Ballistic style pressing of any type must be limited to explosive strength weights ranging from 30 percent to 60 percent. It can be dangerous with larger weights that are used for speed strength, which means weights ranging from 75 percent to 85 percent with the average percent of 80 percent. One can barely touch the chest with a fast eccentric phase then through a fast switch to reversible phase concentrically.

Reversible muscle actions are constantly used in most human movements such as a windup movement during any correct throwing movements. The faster the stretch-shortening cycle, the higher the increase in force and power. We know that reversible muscle action plays a great role in doing landing and takeoffs. All types of throwing require an explosive effort. This means the majority of weight training must also be explosive effort as well.

For a Westside powerlifter in a monthly plan, speed strength training (weights ranging from 75 percent to 85 percent) consists of 100 squats and 80 pulls, while the M-E workout consists of only 12 lifts at 90 percent up to an all time record mostly in special pulls or squats. The pressing workouts consist of the same ratio by percents. All ways use a fast eccentric phase to take advantage of muscle and tendon elasticity. For an example, when an athlete performs depth jumps, he or she is falling at 9.8 m/s. Everyone knows they can be dangerous, but very effective due to kinetic energy. I ask you, why would anyone lower a weight slowly? Eccentrics, especially slow eccentrics, while building larger muscles, also causes most of your muscle pain, something we just don't need.

Throwers are not body builders. Westside recommends perfectly following the optimal number of lifts and reps per workout to avoid overtraining or under training. Weight training should emulate your sport. The throw events require super strength and a massive power. This means the Dynamic Method must be employed when lifting and throwing medicine balls.

Forget heavy or light training, but pay close attention to the movement velocity. Think more on the lines of fast and slow weights. Pay close attention to the percent charts in this chapter on periodization. It will provide the correct force-velocity relationship.

Special Pressing Workouts

First, the Dynamic Method.

During the off season do the maximal number of lifts in the 70 percent up to 80 percent chart.

Example: 400 Max Bench				
Percent	Weight	Reps	Lifts	Volume
75%	300	9x3	24	
80%	320	9x3	24	
85%	340	9x3	24	
				7,200

Special Pressing Workouts

First, do hypertrophy workouts to add muscle mass to the upper body. A proven method is to perform six sets of six reps for 36 total reps. Start moderately so the athlete can add weight for three weeks.

For the second phase, go to eight sets of eight reps for three weeks for a total of 64 reps. To start the eight reps, go back to a weight slightly less than the first week of six reps.

The third and final phase consists of 10 sets of 10 reps for a total of 100 reps, which is high volume training for the non competitive season.

After nine weeks of hypertrophy workouts, you are ready to start the Dynamic Method. In a three-week phase, use 75 percent to 80 and 85 percent going up five percent per week for nine sets of three reps. Use three grips:. The first is with the index finger just touching the smooth part of the bar. Move out two inches for the second grip. For the third grip your little finger should touch the power ring.

Special Note

Try to press the bar in a straight line almost toward your feet. This eliminates most pec injuries as the focus is on the arms, delts and upper back. Always try to push yourself into the bench pad away from the bar. Doing this will activate the upper back. This is very important.

Pin Pressing

Here are two versions to use for speed pressing. The first is to lower the bar to a pin close to your chest. Relax, and then press weight as fast as possible to lock out. The second version calls for the athlete to start the bar off pin concentrically with no eccentric phase. Be sure to line up correctly to prevent injuries. This method can be done seated, standing, flat, incline or decline.

Floor Press

Lie on the floor and lower the bar until your triceps are touching the floor relaxed. Press violently to lock out. Dumbbells can also be used. For more variety, use special bars such as a chamber bar, football bar, or tee bar.

Explosive Strength

All the above exercises can be used for explosive strength. Simply use 30 percent to 50 percent weight to increase velocity. By changing the percent of your one rep max, it changes the special strength you are developing. This covers all pressing including behind the neck, which is a good test for a shot putter.

THROWER'S GUIDE TO STRENGTH TRAINING

Maximal Effort Method

The Maximal Effort Method is lifting or exerting against maximal resistance. This means working up to a one rep max as fast as possible. There is not a five to three or two max. A one rep max builds strength endurance. Remember, you throw an implement one throw at a time. There must be 72 hours between upper body workouts for total recovery. The small special workouts can be every 12 or 24 hours. This accomplishes two vital things—raising work capacity and raising GPP.

Speed Strength and Max Effort Workouts

Here is a list of speed strength and max effort workouts that are intended to be rotated in three-week waves in a multi-year program. While we did not lift, all programs were devised by Medvedev. As you can see, a total of 18 lifts per workout are used, plus you must use a speed strength wave with the squat. The waves cover the snatch, power snatch, snatch pulls, clean and jerk, power clean, and clean pulls. Remember the 20 percent classical or barbell lifts while 80 percent special exercises mentioned before ranging from Goodmornings, pressing, jumping, depth jumps, back raises, reverse hypers, belt squats, leg presses, and many more.

Use the pulling and squatting workouts for max effort, plus pressing and jerking exercises. Other exercises can be found in Supertraining 2003 sixth edition by Mel Siff

Forty Three-Week Wave Examples

- Remember a new three-week dynamic wave begins on the fourth week!

Week	Exercise	Sets	Reps	Lifts	Percent of 1RM
1	Snatch	3	3	9	75%
	Clean	3	3	9	75%
2	Snatch	3	3	9	80%
	Clean	3	3	9	80%
3	Snatch	3	3	9	85%
	Clean	3	3	9	85%

Week	Exercise	Sets	Reps	Lifts	Percent of 1RM
1	Power clean from knees	3	3	9	75%
	Snatch from small box	3	3	9	70%
2	Power clean from knees	3	3	9	80%
	Snatch from high box	3	3	9	75%
3	Power clean from knees	3	3	9	75%
	Snatch from high box	3	3	9	85%

THROWER'S GUIDE TO STRENGTH TRAINING

- Remember a new three-week dynamic wave begins on the fourth week!

Week	Exercise	Sets	Reps	Lifts	Percent of 1RM
1	Classic snatch	3	3	9	75%
	Hang clean	3	3	9	75%
2	Clean pull from floor	3	3	9	80%
	Snatch below the knees	3	3	9	80%
3	Power snatch w/overhead squat	3	3	9	85%
	Hang clean above the knee	3	3	9	85%

Week	Exercise	Sets	Reps	Lifts	Percent of 1RM
1	Power clean from floor	3	3	9	75%
	Split snatch	3	3	9	75%
2	Power clean from floor	3	3	9	80%
	Split snatch	3	3	9	80%
3	Power clean from floor	3	3	9	85%
	Split snatch	3	3	9	85%

- Remember a new three-week dynamic wave begins on the fourth week!

Week	Exercise	Sets	Reps	Lifts	Percent of 1RM
1	Snatch on a low box	3	3	9	75%
	Clean from low box	3	3	9	75%
2	Snatch on a low box	3	3	9	80%
	Clean from low box	3	3	9	80%
3	Snatch on a low box	3	3	9	85%
	Clean from low box	3	3	9	85%

Week	Exercise	Sets	Reps	Lifts	Percent of 1RM
1	Clean and jerk w/barbell at knee	3	3	9	75%
	Snatch pull w/ rise on toes	3	3	9	75%
2	Clean and jerk w/barbell at knee	3	3	9	80%
	Snatch pull w/ rise on toes	3	3	9	80%
3	Clean and jerk w/barbell at knee	3	3	9	85%
	Snatch pull w/ rise on toes	3	3	9	85%

THROWER'S GUIDE TO STRENGTH TRAINING

- Remember a new three-week dynamic wave begins on the fourth week!

Week	Exercise	Sets	Reps	Lifts	Percent of 1RM
1	Hang clean and jerk	3	3	9	75%
	Split snatch	3	3	9	75%
2	Hang clean and jerk	3	3	9	80%
	Split snatch	3	3	9	80%
3	Hang clean and jerk	3	3	9	85%
	Split snatch	3	3	9	85%

Week	Exercise	Sets	Reps	Lifts	Percent of 1RM
1	RDL	3	3	9	75%
	Clean pull to knee level	3	3	9	75%
2	RDL	3	3	9	80%
	Clean pull to knee level	3	3	9	80%
3	RDL	3	3	9	85%
	Clean pull to knee level	3	3	9	85%

- Remember a new three-week dynamic wave begins on the fourth week!

Week	Exercise	Sets	Reps	Lifts	Percent of 1RM
1	Clean pull w/ close grip	3	3	9	75%
	Split snatch w/ bar below knees	3	3	9	75%
2	Clean pull w/ close grip	3	3	9	80%
	Split snatch w/ bar below knees	3	3	9	80%
3	Clean pull w/ close grip	3	3	9	85%
	Split snatch w/ bar below knees	3	3	9	85%

Week	Exercise	Sets	Reps	Lifts	Percent of 1RM
1	Snatch grip deadlift	3	3	9	75%
	Push jerk w/ overhead squat	3	3	9	75%
2	Snatch grip deadlift	3	3	9	80%
	Push jerk w/ overhead squat	3	3	9	80%
3	Snatch grip deadlift	3	3	9	85%
	Push jerk w/ overhead squat	3	3	9	85%

THROWER'S GUIDE TO STRENGTH TRAINING

- Remember a new three-week dynamic wave begins on the fourth week!

Week	Exercise	Sets	Reps	Lifts	Percent of 1RM
1	Hang clean w/ front squat	3	3	9	75%
	Snatch pull followed by classic snatch	3	3	9	75%
2	Hang clean w/ front squat	3	3	9	80%
	Snatch pull followed by classic snatch	3	3	9	80%
3	Hang clean w/ front squat	3	3	9	85%
	Snatch pull followed by classic snatch	3	3	9	85%

Week	Exercise	Sets	Reps	Lifts	Percent of 1RM
1	Snatch pull starting at knees	3	3	9	75%
	Clean pull from below the knees	3	3	9	75%
2	Snatch pull starting at knees	3	3	9	80%
	Clean pull from below the knees	3	3	9	80%
3	Snatch pull starting at knees	3	3	9	85%
	Clean pull from below the knees	3	3	9	85%

Louie Simmons

- Remember a new three-week dynamic wave begins on the fourth week!

Week	Exercise	Sets	Reps	Lifts	Percent of 1RM
1	Classic snatch	3	3	9	75%
	Clean pull from floor	3	3	9	75%
2	Classic snatch	3	3	9	80%
	Clean pull from floor	3	3	9	80%
3	Classic snatch	3	3	9	85%
	Clean pull from floor	3	3	9	85%

Week	Exercise	Sets	Reps	Lifts	Percent of 1RM
1	Power clean to squat to jerk	3	3	9	75%
	Hang snatch pull below the knees	3	3	9	75%
2	Power clean to squat to jerk	3	3	9	80%
	Hang snatch pull below the knees	3	3	9	80%
3	Power clean to squat to jerk	3	3	9	85%
	Hang snatch pull below the knees	3	3	9	85%

THROWER'S GUIDE TO STRENGTH TRAINING

- Remember a new three-week dynamic wave begins on the fourth week!

Week	Exercise	Sets	Reps	Lifts	Percent of 1RM
1	Snatch from above knees	3	3	9	75%
	Jerk from stands	3	3	9	75%
2	Snatch from above knees	3	3	9	80%
	Jerk from stands	3	3	9	80%
3	Snatch from above knees	3	3	9	85%
	Jerk from stands	3	3	9	85%

Week	Exercise	Sets	Reps	Lifts	Percent of 1RM
1	Push jerk from behind neck followed by overhead squat	3	3	9	75%
	Snatch pull followed by classic snatch	3	3	9	75%
2	Push jerk from behind neck followed by overhead squat	3	3	9	80%
	Snatch pull followed by classic snatch	3	3	9	80%
3	Push jerk from behind neck followed by overhead squat	3	3	9	85%
	Snatch pull followed by classic snatch	3	3	9	85%

- Remember a new three-week dynamic wave begins on the fourth week!

Week	Exercise	Sets	Reps	Lifts	Percent of 1RM
1	Split snatch w/ bar at knee level	3	3	9	75%
	Half jerk followed by jerk taken from stand	3	3	9	75%
2	Split snatch w/ bar at knee level	3	3	9	80%
	Half jerk followed by jerk taken from stand	3	3	9	80%
3	Split snatch w/ bar at knee level	3	3	9	85%
	Half jerk followed by jerk taken from stand	3	3	9	85%

Week	Exercise	Sets	Reps	Lifts	Percent of 1RM
1	Clean pull off block	3	3	9	75%
	Hang snatch from above knees	3	3	9	75%
2	Clean pull off block	3	3	9	80%
	Hang snatch from above knees	3	3	9	80%
3	Clean pull off block	3	3	9	85%
	Hang snatch from above knees	3	3	9	85%

THROWER'S GUIDE TO STRENGTH TRAINING

- Remember a new three-week dynamic wave begins on the fourth week!

Week	Exercise	Sets	Reps	Lifts	Percent of 1RM
1	Clean to front squat	3	3	9	75%
	Snatch pull from floor rise onto toes	3	3	9	75%
2	Clean to front squat	3	3	9	80%
	Snatch pull from floor rise onto toes	3	3	9	80%
3	Clean to front squat	3	3	9	85%
	Snatch pull from floor rise onto toes	3	3	9	85%

Week	Exercise	Sets	Reps	Lifts	Percent of 1RM
1	Hang snatch below knees	3	3	9	75%
	Clean pull standing on block	3	3	9	75%
2	Hang snatch below knees	3	3	9	80%
	Clean pull standing on block	3	3	9	80%
3	Hang snatch below knees	3	3	9	85%
	Clean pull standing on block	3	3	9	85%

- Remember a new three-week dynamic wave begins on the fourth week!

Week	Exercise	Sets	Reps	Lifts	Percent of 1RM
1	Clean from blocks below knee	3	3	9	75%
	Snatch pull w/bar at knee level	3	3	9	75%
2	Clean from blocks below knee	3	3	9	80%
	Snatch pull w/bar at knee level	3	3	9	80%
3	Clean from blocks below knee	3	3	9	85%
	Snatch pull w/bar at knee level	3	3	9	85%

Week	Exercise	Sets	Reps	Lifts	Percent of 1RM
1	Split snatch w/overhead squat	3	3	9	75%
	Clean	3	3	9	75%
2	Split snatch w/overhead squat	3	3	9	80%
	Clean	3	3	9	80%
3	Split snatch w/overhead squat	3	3	9	85%
	Clean	3	3	9	85%

THROWER'S GUIDE TO STRENGTH TRAINING

- Remember a new three-week dynamic wave begins on the fourth week!

Week	Exercise	Sets	Reps	Lifts	Percent of 1RM
1	Clean and jerk	3	3	9	75%
	Snatch	3	3	9	75%
2	Clean and jerk	3	3	9	80%
	Snatch	3	3	9	80%
3	Clean and jerk	3	3	9	85%
	Snatch	3	3	9	85%

Week	Exercise	Sets	Reps	Lifts	Percent of 1RM
1	Snatch	3	3	9	75%
	Clean	3	3	9	75%
2	Snatch	3	3	9	80%
	Clean	3	3	9	80%
3	Snatch	3	3	9	85%
	Clean	3	3	9	85%

Note: "Accommodating Resistance Percent" reflects tension at the top or finish position of the movement!

Week	Exercise	Sets	Reps	Lifts	Percent of 1RM	Accommodating Resistance Percent
1	Power clean to push jerk	3	3	9	50%	25%
	Snatch grip deadlift to knees	3	3	9	50%	25%
2	Power clean to push jerk	3	3	9	55%	25%
	Snatch grip deadlift to knees	3	3	9	55%	25%
3	Power clean to push jerk	3	3	9	60%	25%
	Snatch grip deadlift to knees	3	3	9	60%	25%

THROWER'S GUIDE TO STRENGTH TRAINING

Week	Exercise	Sets	Reps	Lifts	Percent of 1RM	Accommodating Resistance Percent
1	Power snatch w/overhead squat	3	3	9	50%	25%
	Hang clean above knee	3	3	9	50%	25%
2	Power snatch w/overhead squat	3	3	9	55%	25%
	Hang clean above knee	3	3	9	55%	25%
3	Power snatch w/overhead squat	3	3	9	60%	25%
	Hang clean above knee	3	3	9	60%	25%

Week	Exercise	Sets	Reps	Lifts	Percent of 1RM	Accommodating Resistance Percent
1	Clean and jerk	3	3	9	50%	25%
	Snatch pull from floor	3	3	9	50%	25%
2	Clean and jerk	3	3	9	55%	25%
	Snatch pull from floor	3	3	9	55%	25%
3	Clean and jerk	3	3	9	60%	25%
	Snatch pull from floor	3	3	9	60%	25%

Louie Simmons

Week	Exercise	Sets	Reps	Lifts	Percent of 1RM	Accommodating Resistance Percent
1	Snatch pull plus snatch pull from below knees plus snatch pull from above knees	3	3	9	50%	25%
	Jerk from behind head	3	3	9	50%	25%
2	Snatch pull plus snatch pull from below knees plus snatch pull from above knees	3	3	9	55%	25%
	Jerk from behind head	3	3	9	55%	25%
3	Snatch pull plus snatch pull from below knees plus snatch pull from above knees	3	3	9	60%	25%
	Jerk from behind head	3	3	9	60%	25%

THROWER'S GUIDE TO STRENGTH TRAINING

Week	Exercise	Sets	Reps	Lifts	Percent of 1RM	Accommodating Resistance Percent
1	Wide grip power clean	3	3	9	50%	25%
	Snatch pull to knees followed by snatch pull overhead	3	3	9	50%	25%
2	Wide grip power clean	3	3	9	55%	25%
	Snatch pull to knees followed by snatch pull overhead	3	3	9	55%	25%
3	Wide grip power clean	3	3	9	60%	25%
	Snatch pull to knees followed by snatch pull overhead	3	3	9	60%	25%

Note: "Accommodating Resistance %" reflects tension at the top or finish position of the movement!

Louie Simmons

Week	Exercise	Sets	Reps	Lifts	Percent of 1RM	Accommodating Resistance Percent
1	RDL	3	3	9	50%	25%
	Push jerk from stands overhead	3	3	9	50%	25%
2	RDL	3	3	9	55%	25%
	Push jerk from stands overhead	3	3	9	55%	25%
3	RDL	3	3	9	60%	25%
	Push jerk from stands overhead	3	3	9	60%	25%

Note: "Accommodating Resistance %" reflects tension at the top or finish position of the movement!

THROWER'S GUIDE TO STRENGTH TRAINING

Week	Exercise	Sets	Reps	Lifts	Percent of 1RM	Accommodating Resistance Percent
1	Power clean to push jerk	3	3	9	50%	25%
	Snatch grip deadlift to knees	3	3	9	50%	25%
2	Power clean to push jerk	3	3	9	55%	25%
	Snatch grip deadlift to knees	3	3	9	55%	25%
3	Power clean to push jerk	3	3	9	60%	25%
	Snatch grip deadlift to knees	3	3	9	60%	25%

Note: "Accommodating Resistance Percent" reflects tension at the top or finish position of the movement!

Louie Simmons

Week	Exercise	Sets	Reps	Lifts	Percent of 1RM	Accommodating Resistance Percent
1	Power snatch w/overhead squat	3	3	9	50%	25%
	Hang clean above knee	3	3	9	50%	25%
2	Power snatch w/overhead squat	3	3	9	55%	25%
	Hang clean above knee	3	3	9	55%	25%
3	Power snatch w/overhead squat	3	3	9	60%	25%
	Hang clean above knee	3	3	9	60%	25%

Note: "Accommodating Resistance %" reflects tension at the top or finish position of the movement!

THROWER'S GUIDE TO STRENGTH TRAINING

Week	Exercise	Sets	Reps	Lifts	Percent of 1RM	Accommodating Resistance Percent
1	Power clean to push jerk	3	3	9	50%	25%
	Snatch grip deadlift to knees	3	3	9	50%	25%
2	Power clean to push jerk	3	3	9	55%	25%
	Snatch grip deadlift to knees	3	3	9	55%	25%
3	Power clean to push jerk	3	3	9	60%	25%
	Snatch grip deadlift to knees	3	3	9	60%	25%

Week	Exercise	Sets	Reps	Lifts	Percent of 1RM	Accommodating Resistance Percent
1	Power snatch w/overhead squat	3	3	9	50%	25%
	Hang clean above knees	3	3	9	50%	25%
2	Power snatch w/overhead squat	3	3	9	55%	25%
	Hang clean above knees	3	3	9	55%	25%
3	Power snatch w/overhead squat	3	3	9	60%	25%
	Hang clean above knees	3	3	9	60%	25%

Note: "Accommodating Resistance Percent" reflects tension at the top or finish position of the movement!

THROWER'S GUIDE TO STRENGTH TRAINING

Week	Exercise	Sets	Reps	Lifts	Percent of 1RM	Accommodating Resistance Percent
1	Clean and jerk	3	3	9	50%	25%
	Snatch pull from floor	3	3	9	50%	25%
2	Clean and jerk	3	3	9	55%	25%
	Snatch pull from floor	3	3	9	55%	25%
3	Clean and jerk	3	3	9	60%	25%
	Snatch pull from floor	3	3	9	60%	25%

Note: "Accommodating Resistance Percent" reflects tension at the top or finish position of the movement!

Louie Simmons

Week	Exercise	Sets	Reps	Lifts	Percent of 1RM	Accommodating Resistance Percent
1	Power snatch standing on block	3	3	9	50%	25%
	Clean pull off blocks	3	3	9	50%	25%
2	Power snatch standing on block	3	3	9	55%	25%
	Clean pull off blocks	3	3	9	55%	25%
3	Power snatch standing on block	3	3	9	60%	25%
	Clean pull off blocks	3	3	9	60%	25%

Note: "Accommodating Resistance Percent" reflects tension at the top or finish position of the movement!

THROWER'S GUIDE TO STRENGTH TRAINING

Week	Exercise	Sets	Reps	Lifts	Percent of 1RM	Accommodating Resistance Percent
1	Power clean w/front squat	3	3	9	50%	25%
	Snatch pull up to knee level	3	3	9	50%	25%
2	Power clean w/front squat	3	3	9	55%	25%
	Snatch pull up to knee level	3	3	9	55%	25%
3	Power clean w/front squat	3	3	9	60%	25%
	Snatch pull up to knee level	3	3	9	60%	25%

Week	Exercise	Sets	Reps	Lifts	Percent of 1RM	Accommodating Resistance Percent
1	Snatch legs straight	3	3	9	50%	25%
	Push jerk from stands	3	3	9	50%	25%
2	Snatch legs straight	3	3	9	55%	25%
	Push jerk from stands	3	3	9	55%	25%
3	Snatch legs straight	3	3	9	60%	25%
	Push jerk from stands	3	3	9	60%	25%

Note: "Accommodating Resistance %" reflects tension at the top or finish position of the movement!

Week	Exercise	Sets	Reps	Lifts	Percent of 1RM	Accommodating Resistance Percent
1	Power clean from knees	3	3	9	50%	25%
	Snatch from high box	3	3	9	50%	25%
2	Power clean from knees	3	3	9	55%	25%
	Snatch from high box	3	3	9	55%	25%
3	Power clean from knees	3	3	9	60%	25%
	Snatch from high box	3	3	9	60%	25%

THROWER'S GUIDE TO STRENGTH TRAINING

Special Notes: Progress is based on Periodization

A weightlifter has to build a strong back and legs to reach the top. I had read David Rigeat could squat 10 reps with 675 pounds at 198-pound body weight. I had also read a story after bombing out of a major meet with a 352-pound snatch. David took some time off. But when he returned to a lifting hall, a lifter was snatching the same 352 pounds that he bombed out with. David's friend noticed he was glaring at the bar and realized what David was thinking and said "don't do it!" David (in street clothes) approached the bar loaded with 352 pounds and proceeded to snatch it with no warm-up. These two stories tell the author just how strong his legs and back were. This could account for David breaking world records.

I have had several novice weightlifters visit Westside to train. By the author's system of combinations of method training, they will break their record in the clean or snatch nine out of 10 times in just 30 minutes. Many times they have been stuck for months without a PR. After setting a new clean or snatch record, which is low by any standards due to low back strength, they are unable to recover from the clean (due to even lower leg strength).

You must raise max strength to reach the top. Many think that speed is most important due to the fact that you can only make the lift with the amount of weight you do in the weakest portion of the lift. It does no good to clean 400 pounds if your front squat is 360 pounds or to snatch 300 pounds if your overhead squat is 280 pounds. The legs must have an over-abundance of strength compared to your clean or snatch. I constantly hear that the squat only has to be a small percent of your clean and jerk. This is completely WRONG! Not only do you have to recover from the clean, but you also have a reserve of leg strength for the thrust in the jerk.

Weightlifters in the former Soviet Union had a wide base before weight training began.

This lead to at least basic leg strength. A good coach or lifter should know that the top five inter-dependent correlations for maximal results are:

1. Power Clean
2. Power Snatch
3. Clean
4. Overhead Squat
5. Clean from the Hang

This is according to *Managing the Training of Weightlifters*.

The author's findings have concluded that when the squat is raised, the pulls and any pull increase as well. So what is the answer? It has been said that some lifters squat six times a week, but with no great results. The author has viewed several squat workouts and found they are too slow to produce proper force. The percentages should range between 75 percent and 85 percent with only barbell weight or 50 percent to 60 percent with 25 percent band tension at the top for three-week pendulum waves. The bar should move at .8 to .9 m/s—this is force equals mass times acceleration. I hope this sounds familiar as it is Newton's Second Law of F=MA Why is this so important? Let's look at the definition of work:

In physics, work is defined as the product of net force and the displacement throughout where that force is exerted or W=Force. If work is a barbell lift, clean, or squat, then how can one move the same or larger weight faster? The answer: by becoming more powerful. In physics, power is divided by the time used to do the work or P=wt. This simply means the more powerful lifter can do the work in less time. Now we are finally getting to the point. Yes, we need a stronger squat! But squatting repeatedly is not the answer. The problem is the Law of Accommodation: meaning if one does the same exercise with the same training load repeatedly, the performance will decrease over time. Many would think this is the definition of insanity, but science refers to it as accommodation, a biological law.

The pulls are the same. They, too, will stop increasing poundages if done repeatedly. The Westside conjugate system calls for breaking down the squats and pulls into segments. You must increase leg strength—meaning calves, hamstrings, and quads—into special exercises for each muscle group.

Special Exercises:
- Leg Presses
- Step Ups
- Glute/Ham Raises
- Inverse Curls
- Calf Raises
- Sled Pulls
- Wheel Barrows
- Back Raises
- Goodmornings
- Reverse Hypers
- Belt Squats
- Box Jumping
- Upright Rows
- Bent Over Rows
- Pullups

These are some small special exercises that can make an incredible difference in building a strong squat and pull.

Why does Westside want you to use a wide stance for squatting? Because you have never worked those muscles! Those unused muscles are contributing to lifting more weight. Wide-stance straight-leg-style deadlifts and wide-stance arched-back power cleans are other examples.

Side Note: I was having a discussion about the deadlift for Olympic lifters when a well known author said that a powerlifting deadlift would not work for an Olympic lifter due to the round backed style. I replied "what about the sumo style where the back is arched?" He had no clue. This is the problem with most (not all) Olympic coaches—they do not have a clue about anything that can improve strength. Perfect form must be taught in the early stages then a constant increase in strength must come to win bigger and bigger contests. I hope this makes sense to you. Hardly anyone has a perfect body for any sport, especially weightlifting. Everyone has some muscle groups stronger than others. Some have very strong backs and not so strong legs. Of course, the back will do the majority of the work load. But what if that individual builds his or her legs up to match their back strength? They could, of course, lift heavier weights and be much safer, too, because the work would be distributed throughout the body.

I have asked Tom Eiseman (780 at 181 pounds) where he felt the deadlift the most and his reply was very profound. His answer was "everywhere." Only small special exercises can bring up lacking or weak muscle groups. An example is ab work. If one did no direct ab work, abs would be weak leading to back ailments. If you are very strong, but slow, you must work on your explosive and speed strength. But don't neglect your strength speed—the one thing you are blessed with. Train what you don't have. But, remember, it does no good to be strong in the wrong exercises.

If Medvedev had more than 75 barbell exercises for the weightlifter, there were of course many more small special exercises. For a single muscle group, many were on special machines; then there are Kettlebells, alternating close grips for snatches and wide grips for cleans, to name a few.

Last, but not least, please read. I have a large list of books for anyone who will read them. I used this material to build the strongest powerlifting gym in the history of powerlifting. As of July 2014, Westside had five of the top 10 totals of all time. This includes the highest total of 3,005 at 271 and the top two coefficient totals of all time. Plus, the number one women's coefficient total of all time. Also, the top coefficient squats for men and women and the top coefficient bench press for men and women in a power meet. This Westside Method is 33 years in the making. Its methods are from weightlifting and track and field.

The author re-engineered the Soviet System to fit not only powerlifting, but all sports. **Warning:** there is no such thing as five rep systems, three rep systems, or the single rep system, nor the Cube Method, 5-3-1 Method or the Nebraska System. These systems are fantasy.

There are four systems that are proven by science:

1. The Maximal Effort Method
2. The Dynamic Effort Method
3. The Sub maximal Effort Method
4. The Repeated Effort Method

Westside thanks the great former Soviet Union sports scientists like V.M Zatsiorsky, and Dr. Mel Siff of *Supertraining* fame (a good friend may he rest in peace) Along with Y.V Verkhoshansky, Mel was a true genius in the development of sports science. And don't forget Dr. Isaac Newton the father of the laws of motion. Without these great men and a long list of others that are mentioned in the references, we wouldn't be where we are today.

Chapter 4
The Conjugate System

Westside has used the Conjugate System since 1970. The Conjugate System's main purpose is to raise a lagging motor system for improving specific motor abilities. It is an alternative to Block Periodization, which is really outdated compared to a Pendulum Wave System. The Pendulum Wave System is used not only for weightlifters, but also for team sports that want to maintain a certain level of strength.

The Pendulum Wave uses repeated, three-week segments for speed strength with weights in the 75 percent to 85 percent range or for explosive strength where the weights are in the 30 percent to 50 percent range. Simply raise the barbell weights five percent each week from 75 to 80 to 85 percent for speed strength or from 30 to 40 to 50 percent for explosive strength.

While Block Periodization calls for using stand-alone general exercises for strength and endurance, with the Conjugate System, general exercises for strength and endurance are done concurrently with technical training to improve technical skill. With Block Periodization the next block after general exercises is directed exercise and then, finally, sport-specific exercise for the competition phase.

The Conjugate System allows for whatever special exercise is needed at that time. The Law of Accommodation is completely avoided by changing the volume and intensity as well as switching the bars every three weeks.

The Max-Effort (M-E) Method is trained during the same week and makes it possible to train all three velocities. Training all three velocities is necessary to build explosive, speed and strength speed.

The Conjugate System was first used with only high level athletes, but Westside has always started beginners training the Conjugate System. The Westside Method trains by the Percent Method. This means that a 400-pound squatter and an 800-pound squatter will move the same percents at the same speed. A person who squats 400 pounds will do half the volume of an 800-pound squatter with the Westside Percent Method. It works for any barbell lift, or also jumping, and should apply to any total workload.

The Conjugate System calls for exchanging special exercises during training. Special exercises range from large barbell exercise to small special exercise like extensions for the knee, back and elbows that are done with a smaller weight barbell or dumbbell as well as specially designed machines that develop a single joint movement.

While resistance training covers a large part of the Conjugate System, the system is used to raise the developmental level of all abilities of the specific motor system that causes one to improve all motor abilities. The more things one can master, the greater the athletic goals one can conquer.

The Westside version of M-E does not call for providing a weekly or monthly plan, but rather possibly choosing the workout at a 6 am breakfast for the 7 am workout. No one has a crystal ball. No one can know what you may need or where your strength or speed level will be in a hypothetical 10-week or 12-week program. With a standard method of block training, it is just a hypothetical guess where you will be in 12 weeks or any time period.

Are you strong enough, fast enough, or explosive enough when you are supposed to be? If you lack one of the qualities, you fail. The Westside version allows the coach and athlete to fully understand where his or her levels of strength, speed endurance and technique stand at any given time of the year. During a weekly plan the athlete analyzes his or her speed or explosive strength on Dynamic Day, how strong he or she is on M-E Day as well as the overall fitness level to prevent injury by working on all large muscle groups with small special single-joint exercises.

As you can see, the Westside Periodization is constant, never broken. It is a multi-year system of combining the Dynamic, M-E and "Repetitions to near Failure" inside all weekly plans.

There are countless workouts to use for the upper and lower body not only with weights, but bands and chains for accommodating resistance, which can also include some special machines with some form of mechanical feedback. As with the weight training, there are many special jumping exercises to rotate for weekly and monthly programs that evolve into yearly and multi-year plans.

Do not forget General Physical Preparedness! (GPP)

At first will be general fitness, but most turn to more directed fitness that encompasses your sport. Long distance running will have no value for a football player. It will build only a base to run slower, not faster. With a 21-day time period, the long distance running ability will deteriorate if not maintained full-time. For explosive sports, work only on increasing acceleration. On the other hand, block-style training is divided into specific blocks of training that in theory will stop progress.

It is not advisable to strength train for six months and then to throw the shot or hammer for the other six months. Furthermore, it is not advisable to strength train for six months and run for the other six months. If strength training is important, why stop doing it? But, rather, it should be altered during the competition phase.

When the athlete stops training after the competition phase, their technique in their specialty deteriorates. The loss of special strength training or loss of specialized technique should not be acceptable. Both strength and technique should be at its zenith during the competition phase.

Avoiding this loss can only happen by training both strength and technique—it must be addressed all year long to some extent. To do this the Conjugate System is the answer as all special training for strength, fitness and technique are being increased constantly by rotating the amount of specialized activities such as strength, GPP and technique work. This is how the requirements of all athletes from novice to highly qualified men and women are acquired.

The Conjugate System is complex, but yet easy to administer. The theory is simple—everything works, but nothing works forever. It is based on accumulated after-effects of all revolving exercises and loads. Most of the work is unidirectional, which completely avoids the Law of Accommodation while simultaneously contributing to raise motor potential and perfect technical skills.

For more information, read *Supertraining* by Dr. Mel Siff (2003).

Chapter 5
Accommodating Resistance

The theory of accommodating resistance is about finding ways to develop the maximal tension throughout the entire range of motion. Any sport movement that has a start must also have a finish. This means that after the acceleration phase there must be a deceleration phase. For the thrower, the release phase is most important due to the relationship between force and posture strength curves. It depends on the body's posture, which means the joint angles.

There have been several machines that provide accommodating resistance throughout the full range of motion. Zander was the first to explore the idea in 1897. Zander developed several strength machines based on Accommodating Resistance. Others throughout history have done so, such as Arthur Allen Jones and his Nautilus-type equipment. Both were based on the human strength curve. But there was and still is a problem—machines will build muscle, not motion. So, what is the answer? To do isokinetic work only on the concentric phase. This device has no reversible muscle action.

Louie Simmons

Reversible Muscular Action

Reversible muscular action or eccentrics is natural as concentric action in all sports. Muscle and tendon elasticity plays a large role in motor output in sports movements due to the stretch-shortening cycle. Westside began using chains hooked to the bar in the late 1980s or early 1990s. This provided accommodating resistance on the concentric phase and had a great impact on not only Westside Barbell, but all sports teams that emulated Westside's system.

But how could the eccentric phase benefit? The answer came from two men: Dick Hartzel and Dave Williams. Dick Hartzel used rubber bands for mostly stretching and resistance training, but by using only band tension it provided zero resistance in the start of a lift. My good friend and coach Dave Williams of Liberty University asked to experiment with rubber bands to help his teams. After using the bands for one and one-half years, Westside found the correct calculations for the combinations of resistance method. So what percentage of barbell weight and band tension? There must be band tension at the bottom or the start of any movement.

With a barbell alone, it can be too heavy to start strongly from the start or too light at the lockout causing a deceleration phase. And, remember, bands would only provide a little resistance at the start. By using bands over the barbell, a perfect amount of resistance is now possible from the start to lockout. It also provides the over-speed eccentrics that can increase reversible muscle actions by using the muscle and tendon elasticity to maximize the reversible muscular actions. For throwers, bands can increase the force on the final step rotation and, most importantly, the release. Placing bands on your barbell or using a band around the body and holding dumbbells or doing pushups will maximize your training for any special strength that requires one particular velocity.

The author has many years of accommodating resistance training experience with the strongest and most powerful athletes in the world. Elastic bands play a large role in the Westside System for increasing special strength by using the correct band percentage to affect a special strength. For building strength speed or slow strength, the bar velocity is slowed by using at least 50 percent of the load using band tension.

An example: A. J. Roberson performed a box squat with 700 pounds of band tension and 510 pounds of barbell weight. This equals 1,210 pounds at lockout. This resulted in a 1,205-pound squat. For A. J.'s speed strength training the ratio was 50 percent, 55 percent and 60 percent barbell weight in a three-week wave with approximately 25 percent band tension, which is 300 pounds band tension. To reach the strength speed max, seven lifts were performed. After warming up, two by two weights were done, then three singles to reach a new max. Just like a weight or powerlifting contest.

For speed strength, 18 lifts are optimal at 70 percent weights and 15 lifts at 80 percent. This data comes from A. S. Prilepin's 1974 research. For speed strength, the barbell velocity is roughly 0.8 m/s.

For explosive strength, the barbell weight is limited to 30 percent to 50 percent with 25 percent band tension at top. The optimal lifts for explosive strength are 36 lifts. This data comes from the author's research with NFL ball players and Olympic Track and Field athletes, both male and female.

You may think that using band tension is very close to accelerated power metrics (AP). AP uses a falling body that causes an increase in kinetic energy (K-E) during the amortization phase. With band tension the greater force is created by external elastic tension.

Reactive Methods

The Soviets were the first to use a method to build reversible strength. They used an apparatus that would detach itself from the barbell after it was lowered eccentrically. With a total of 80 percent total weight and 20 percent on the weight releasers, the athlete would then quickly move concentrically to full recovery for the development of speed and explosive strength. This method is commonly known as Load Releasers.

Heavy-Light Set

Yuri Verkhoshansky and other top Soviet sport experts would load a barbell with a load of 90 percent for one or two reps, then rest 10 to 15 seconds and lift 70 percent with as much speed as possible. This stimulates the central nervous system to produce a powerful contraction with the smaller weight.

Static-Dynamic Method

This method calls for a barbell to be loaded to a resistance that cannot be overcome. After pulling or pushing for one or two reps, it can increase dynamic strength and explosive strength of a subsequent action as a result of the after-effect phenomenon.

These last two methods can make or break the athlete due to holding the static load too long or acquiring too much muscular fatigue with too short of a rest interval. While the above two methods are very effective, there is advice that is far superior to either.

Introducing the Static Dynamic DeveloperTM

The Static Dynamic Developer makes it possible to produce an isometric contraction for a set time limit of mostly one to three seconds with a predetermined amount of resistance that distinguishes what velocity the barbell will move it that reflexes what special strength is being imposed.

The two studies below will further explain the functions of this incredible training device.

It is very important to use several special strength methods to enhance sports mastery. The athlete must overcome new barriers for many years. The Conjugate System is in order as it offers a series of builders that move close to the velocity of the tester that is used in competition.

If your technique is correct and you break your box squat, high pull, overhead shot test and throw from the front of the circle, you should be able to break your shot put distance.

Plyometrics is just one method that describes shock method training as shown in *Supertraining* (Siff, 2003).

Everything works, but nothing works forever, while some special exercises are completely wrong for some. This must be discussed by the coach and athlete.

Following experimentation with the Static Dynamic Developer by Louie Simmons and Shobit Jain at Westside Barbell, Columbus, Ohio, Shobit Jain offers the following review.

Louie Simmons
Static Dynamic Developer

By Shobit Jain

Static dynamic developer exercise equipment has two variations: 1) a Smith machine variation, and 2) a cable-pulley variation, which was used in the project. The Smith machine variation can be used to perform movements such as squat jumps, deadlifts, clean and jerk, power cleans, clean and snatch, and other compound movements. The cable-pulley station variation is designed to perform single-joint exercises such as seated hamstring curls, triceps extensions, some multi-joint exercises such as seated back rows, lat pull-downs, and exercises mimicking the motions of baseball pitching, bat swing for baseball, golf, cricket, and tennis, and sports involving rotational movements of the body such as javelin throw, short put, and the like.

The Static-Dynamic Developer can be utilized to perform explosive static-dynamic exercises in which isometric and explosive dynamic strength efforts are alternated. The goal here is to achieve high central nervous system stimulation. The exercise execution method, used to perform static-dynamic exercises (Verkhoshansky, 1984), is divided into two phases, the isometric phase and the dynamic phase. In the isometric phase there is an isometric tension against an external opposition—in this study, the weight (30 percent to 50 percent of a one rep max, or 80 percent) held static by an electric circuit creates "higher central nervous system excitability" (Verkhoshansky, 1984). The second phase (dynamic phase) involves sudden elimination of the weak external resistance resulting in an instantaneous explosive muscle contraction.

What is the science behind it, you ask?

We know that the cross-bridge cycling that involves cross-bridge formation between actins and myosin filaments results in skeletal muscle contractions. When a muscle is under active tension with no visible movement, isometric force is higher than that during normal isometric contraction (without external resistance). We also know that when the Central Nervous System (CNS)—composed of the brain and spinal cord—is stimulated, its efferent division carries information out of the nervous system to the periphery. This action innervates the skeletal muscle fibers, which in turn result in the contraction of skeletal muscle. Thus, the higher the CNS stimulation, the more the muscle fibers are recruited (Kenny, 1982). Explosive movements require maximum recruitment of skeletal muscle fibers. Thus, significant nervous stimulation is essential. If appropriate signals do not originate from the CNS, the maximum effort necessary for the explosive movements will not occur.

Also, according to Newton's 2nd law—***Force=Mass x Acceleration***—to lift more load (mass), the athletes should be able to generate more force, which requires higher CNS stimulation (achieved during isometric phase). A higher CNS stimulation results in more motor unit activation. The athletes must be able to generate more force to move the weight implement at high speed in order to complete the movement in time (more acceleration), which requires the athletes to be explosive. This is because the CNS can be stimulated only for a certain period of time, which means that motor units can be activated only for a certain period. This is the goal in the isometric phase of the movement, i.e. high CNS stimulation. Once the athletes adapt with high CNS stimulation at the joint angles corresponding to sticking points, their ability to produce force at that joint angle improves and thus they are able to lift heavier loads.

In the isometric phase of the exercise, an individual is required to exert as much force as possible against an immovable load that results in higher CNS excitability and higher recruitment of motor units and thereby higher muscle fiber activation (Kenny, 1982). An increased muscle fiber activation in the isometric phase causes the dynamic phase to be more explosive. Moreover, isometric tension executed in a given joint angle results in a specific training effect: increased force effort expressed with the same joint angle. It also causes a "collateral training effect for the forced effort expressed in other joint angles" (Verkhoshansky, 1982). It thus helps in increasing the strength capabilities of muscle(s) involved in the main competition movement.

Moreover, if we look from the engineering standpoint, viscoelastic structures such as tendons with increased stiffness (Young's Modulus) have higher load bearing capacity (stress), i.e. they can handle more load without undergoing elongation to failure (reduced strain). Also, tendons with higher stiffness have higher energy storage capacity (Kubo et. al. 2017). We know that tendons contribute to the explosive muscular contractions by transmitting force generated by muscle fibers to the bone. During the isometric phase of the movement, the force exerted by the muscle fibers produce a stretch in tendons that leads to a high amount of potential energy being stored in the muscle-tendon unit. This high-energy storage thus leads to increased stiffness of tendons and decreased elongation at a given force level, resulting in reduced risk of injury (Blackburn 2014, Kubo et. al. 2017, Swantesson et. al. 1998).

From the coaching standpoint, it is a great tool for developing starting strength. We all know that to move a weight with sufficient velocity, one must have adequate starting strength, which is defined as the ability to turn on as many muscle fibers as possible instantaneously. Most athletes lack starting strength, which prevents them from lifting more weight that they are capable of. This is due to insufficient motor unit recruitment in muscle group(s). By exerting highest amount force against an immovable resistance (isometric contraction) the athletes learn to recruit sufficient motor units and thus their starting strength increases. Also, as mentioned earlier, the more the motor unit recruitment, the more the dynamic phase is going to be explosive. Thus, by training with this equipment one can develop isometric strength, starting strength, and explosive strength and thus absolute strength.

If you look at the strength curve with force as ordinate and time as abscissa, you will see that when one goes from an eccentric contraction to concentric contraction, there is a phase in between the two called Transition Phase or Amortization Phase, which looks like a "trough" of a sinusoidal wave. The goal is to get a steeper rise in the upward curve, i.e. starting strength. For this, one needs to have a shorter amortization phase that in turn requires great static strength. The steeper the upward curve, the more the increment in starting strength and explosive strength as well as more are one's chances of increasing the maximum force (F_{max}) and equating it with absolute strength. Moreover, a steeper upward curve will also result in attainment of maximum force in least possible time (explosive strength).

By working on the Static Dynamic Developer, one can increase static strength, which shortens the amortization phase and thus enables one to achieve a steep rise in upward curve. Therefore, one is able to increase explosive strength as well as absolute strength. This, in my opinion, is the best way to improve performance, especially in sports such as powerlifting where the objective is to raise the absolute strength.

How to use it?

One can use this machine in between the sets of the main movement when the athlete is attempting to break his/her personal record. One can also use it as an accessory, but be sure to not overdo it as it can stop the athlete's progress. You can use the equipment in both ways as well, i.e. in between the sets of the main movement and as an accessory movement.

To use it between the sets of the main movement, say for example the bench press, the coach will first allow the athlete to try to break his/her own personal record. While the athlete is attempting the maximal effort press, the coach must carefully observe the joint angle(s) at which sticking point occurs that might result in failure attempt. The coach will then have the athlete use the Static Dynamic equipment. The isometric contraction should occur at the joint angle corresponding to the sticking point followed by the dynamic movement static phase ends. Perform four repetitions with 10 seconds of rest between sets. Also, make sure the isometric phase lasts for about three to six seconds and no longer or shorter than that, else it either won't have a carry-over to the main movement or it can tax the CNS too much, which can actually take the athlete's progress backward. Once four repetitions are done, the athlete takes 10 to 15 seconds rest and goes back to attempting the bench press PR.

One of the athletes in my study had failed with the concentric pin press PR attempt while using 170 pounds with the sticking point at approximately 110 degrees elbow joint angle (0 degrees being completely extended elbow joint). The athlete performed rope triceps extensions isometric holds at approximately 110 degrees according to the protocol mentioned earlier, followed by the dynamic phase. The athlete then again attempted the PR weight and lifted the weight easily, i.e. the athlete was able to accelerate through the range of motion, which is an indicator of increased explosive strength as explosive strength is also displayed in the form of acceleration. Why? Because at that elbow joint angle, the isometric holds caused an increase in the CNS stimulation and hence the motor unit recruitment threshold increased thereby eliminating the sticking point. Moreover, the PR attempt was much more explosive as compared to what it was before due to the dynamic phase that follows the isometric contraction phase.

To use the equipment as an accessory, the coach must use it at the end of the workout or as the last exercise for the weak muscle group—triceps in this case. Have the athlete perform isometric holds at multiple joint angles in a single repetition to eliminate all the possible sticking points that might be present in the range of motion. Perform four repetitions in a similar manner. The rest period between repetitions can be 20 to 30 seconds to enable the athlete's CNS to recover from the previous rep (I also did experiment with rest intervals ranging between five and 20 seconds as well as 30 and two minutes with average results, which emphasizes the importance of optimal rest periods for recovery.)

Four repetitions constitute one round. Perform two rounds when using the equipment as an accessory and one round when using it in between main movement sets. One can use bands or weights or a combination of bands and weights. The combination of bands and weight is preferred due to its ability to change and optimize the force-velocity curve. The coach should also take feedback from the athlete after each repetition about the intensity of the movement on the Rate of Perceived Exertion (RPE) scale and try to give cues to the athlete like "Keep pushing," "More force," etc.

To sum it up, this equipment not only increases that rate of force development, but also can be used to improve strength capabilities at certain joint angles at which the athlete is the weakest while at the same time reducing the risk of injury by increasing tissue stillness and eliminating the sticking points thus improving performance.

Louie Simmons

All the best,

Shobit Jain

Shobit Jain is the CEO of A. S. Engineering, established in 2018 at Nagpur, Maharashtra, India. They are a manufacturer and wholesale trader of premium quality chest press machines, dumbbells, ankle weights, battle ropes, and the like.

References

Blackburn, J. Troy, and Marc F. Norcross. "The effects of isometric and isotonic training on hamstring stiffness and anterior cruciate ligament loading mechanisms." *Journal of Electromyography and Kinesiology* 24. 1 (2014): 98-103.

Kenney, W. Larry, Jack Wilmore, and David Costill. *Physiology of Sport and Exercise 6th Edition*. Human Kinetics, 2015.

Kubo, Keitaro, Tomonobu Ishigaki, and Toshihiro Ikebukuro. "Effects of Plyometric and Isometric Training on Muscle and Tendon Stiffness in Vivo." *Physiological Reports* 5.15 (3017): e13374. PMC Web. 16 Nov. 2017.

Svantesson, U., et al. "Comparison of muscle and tendon stiffness, jumping ability muscle strength and fatigue in the plantar flexors." *Scandinavian journal of medicine and science in sports* 8.5 (1998): 252-256.

Verkhoshansky, Yuri, and Natalia Verkhoshansky. *Special strength training: manual for coaches*. Rome: Verkhoshansky Sstm, 2011.

Chapter 6
Explosive Strength through Jumping

I will always remember what my friend, four-time Olympian Hammer Thrower Jud Logan told me about his experience with the Germans and the effects of jumping on his hammer throwing. His power clean had gone from 402 pounds to 440 pounds along with the pressing and squatting, but had no effect on increasing the distance of his throws. When he discussed this problem with his German track and field friends they suggested jumping. After a while, his box jump increased to 56 inches for five sets of five jumps at a body weight of 285 pounds. And his throws began to increase as well. This lesson has never escaped by mind to this day.

I realized then that jumping plays an important role in a thrower's special training. But, first, the athlete must be prepared to add special jumping into his or her training. I wrote a book in 2007 with an accompanying CD that covers all aspects of building explosive strength through a series of special jumping from the basic fundamentals to the most advanced methods to increase explosive strength. I was highly influenced by three experts in the field of developing explosive strength through jumping: Tadeusz Starzynski, Henryk Solansky, and Andrzej Lasocki.

It is of no benefit to become stronger if you become slower. This can cause a negative result in your throwing.

What is explosive strength? By definition it is the ability to rapidly increase force (Tidow, 1990). Tidow says the steeper the increase of strength in time, the greater your explosive strength.

The ability to jump well depends on many things including body weight, body type (meaning the athlete's proportions), speed, strength, and how much elasticity the muscles use during the take-out phase. It is possible to measure your jumping ability by jumping on a higher box or a longer distance. Westside prefers to jump on boxes that are of a solid nature to eliminate inhibitions the athlete may have.

Since this book is for throwers and not jumpers, only general jumping exercises will be discussed and shown. To prepare the thrower for a complete jumping program, start with a series of seated exercises.

Seated Exercises

- Sitting barbell presses
- Sitting barbell curls (Dumbbells or Kettlebells also can be used.)

Kneeling Exercises

- Kneeling arm curls
- Kneeling barbell presses

- Kneeling squats with barbell
- Kneeling squats with barbell jump-out to knees
- Kneeling clean
- Kneeling clean jumping onto feet
- Kneeling snatch
- Kneeling snatch jumping onto feet
- Kneeling split snatch
- Kneeling split snatch jumping onto feet

Resistance Jumps on Boxes

- Box jump with barbell on one box
- Box jump landing on two boxes
- Box jump with weight vest
- Box jump with ankle weights
- Box jump with Kettlebells
- Box jump with combinations of resistance, meaning more than one type of resistance.

Methods for Box Jumping

1. Jump down from box to higher box
2. Jump after a two- to three-step approach
3. Sit on a box, rock back, then jump on higher box
4. Jump out of foam pad or sand
5. Single-leg jumping
6. Jump sideways

This approach is for long-term planning that allows you to rotate jump methods when you feel no more progress can be made. By not fully adapting to a single method of jumping you will avoid accommodation. The many methods of jumping will also increase movement skills. The coach and athlete will determine what methods of jumping will bring the best results to raise your level of strength, speed and coordination, which will carry over to the throwing events. Most experience best results by performing 40 jumps two times a week.

Squatting and pulling will build the foundation for special jumping. Try a record every 21 days. Break records by small amounts of two or three inches. This should be optimal progress for most.

For general jumping ability, jump off and on even boxes. For building strength in eccentric actions, use a higher box to lower box. For building strength in concentric actions, use lower box to higher box. With no resistance, the advanced thrower can use 120 jumps at times outside the throwing season.

Special Note

Jumping up can be very taxing if you are not fit. Depth jumps can be much harder on the athlete due to absorbing the load elasticity. The amortization should be as short as possible. The thrower must know how to land correctly to prevent injuries. At some point when doing depth jumps there is a height of the drop that goes from building explosive to absolute strength—normally at 36 inches. This is due to a slow amortization phase. When landing you develop maximum strength at the precise angle you land. This can be referred to as accentuation training. Here you land in only the angle where the demand for high force production is maximal.

Depth Jumps

Depth jumps can be very strenuous and may cause injury. There are many things to consider when doing depth jumps, such as body weight, the height of the fall, and knowing how to land. In landing, the task of the athlete is to first absorb the landing eccentrically, then as fast as possible jump upward. The strength building is through kinetic energy. Knowing that depth jumps can be very stressful, it is advisable to perform drop jumps. This requires the athlete to drop off a box from a higher and higher height. By doing this, the coach will find the optimal height the thrower can absorb safely.

Depth jumps must be done correctly. After landing immediately rebound as high as possible onto a box or jump upward and touch a hanging ball or some type of object.

Depth Jump Guidelines

1. Minimal amortization phase
2. Must have high level of GPP to start
3. After landing, jump as high as possible
4. Do not depth jump if pain or fatigued muscles are present
5. Limit depth jumps to one or two times per week
6. Novice throwers limit total jumps to 24 per workout
7. Advanced throwers can do 40 jumps two times per week
8. When performing depth jumps, reduce some amount of squatting or pulling during M-E training.
9. Depth jumping should not be done any less than 72 hours from working technique.
10. Depth jumps, while very taxing, have no equal in building explosive strength

confirmed by countless studies.

More information can be found in *Fundamentals of Special Strength-Training in Sport*, by Y. V. Verkhoshansky.

By only jumping up onto a box, Westside has produced a 55-inch box jump by an 18-year-old girl named Shalom Conley; a 63 ½-inch box jump by Joe Pierce; and a 66-inch box jump by Jaden Lacaria. I highly suggest you study the works of Y. V. Verkhoshansky and Nicolai Bernstein.

References

Supertraining, Mel C. Siff

Special Strength Training Manual for Coaches, Yuri and Natalia Verkhoshansky

Fundamentals of Special Strength-Training in Sport, Yuri Verkhoshansky

Science and Practice of Strength Training, V.M. Zatsiorsky and William J. Kraemer

Science of Sports Training, Thomas Kurz

Explosive Power and Jumping Ability, Tadeusz Starzynski and Henryk Sozansky

The World Atlas of Exercises for Track and Field

Chapter 7
Transition Weight Training from Off Season to Competition Period

During the off season for a thrower, the objective is to become stronger and more powerful. During this time, all lifts must be increased, meaning the pulls, squat, bench presses and pushes behind the head. As the lifts go up, you are, of course, stronger. But, it is just as important that your box jumps go up as well as this provides an indication of how powerful you are. It is simple. If your box jumps go up you are more powerful. If your box jumps go down, your power is going down as well. The same is true for long jumping.

Recently we raised a shot putter's squat from 770 pounds to 915 pounds in nine weeks in the off season. His high pulls increased from 440 pounds to 495 pounds for three reps. It was measured by sitting pins in a power rack at chest level, touching the pins on each rep. The bench press was 530 pounds touch and go off the chest.

THROWER'S GUIDE TO STRENGTH TRAINING

Joe Kovacs notes that it is not advisable to stop all throwing in the off season while your strength and power is increased. Your throwing technique will deteriorate. Strength and sports technique must be raised simultaneously.

The track and field community must stop block periodization and move into the modern world of wave periodization and the Conjugate System where all facets of sports training is trained in the same weekly plan. It makes it possible to monitor your strength, power, technique, fitness and recovery.

Once the season starts, the emphasis is on maintaining the squat and not trying to improve it, but at the same time increasing the push behind the head and push up the bench off pads held on the chest. The most efficient method to maintain a squat—say 800 pounds—is to use the three-week wave system that Westside has used to produce 92 men with squats over 800-pounds.

For speed strength, the percentage should range from 75 percent to 85 percent in a three-week wave. This data is from A. D. Ermakov's and N. S. Atanasov's research with 780 highly qualified weightlifters.

During the season, use the optimal number of lifts, which are five sets of five reps according to the data from A. S. Prilepin's research as the Russian weight lifting coach from 1975 to 1985.

The squats should use the Combinations of Resistance Method. The bar weight would be 400 to 440 pounds and 480 pounds plus 25 percent band tension at lockout done off a parallel box with a wide stance and with focus on pushing your feet out to the sides to produce the greatest force. The bar speed must be .8/ms or higher to produce the desired effect. But by using 400 pounds to 480 pounds plus bands, it will produce 800 pounds of force—this is Newton's 2nd Law that states that force is proportional to the rate of change in momentum (F=ma). During the season when training for acceleration is paramount, this is the most effective method to use. M-E training is not recommended as it is slow velocity training. Speed strength is performed at intermediate velocity.

After the speed strength squats, you should do 40 box jumps two times a week to measure your power development. Box or long jumping after this is a Contrast Method, which is a measure of explosive strength. Explosive strength is the ability to apply a maximum force in minimum time, a key component in speed strength sports.

Everything for the legs should be high velocity training. After squatting and jumping, pick a lower back hamstring exercise like Reverse Hypers or do back raises or calf-ham-glute raises.

Two workouts for the bench press should both be extreme—one for explosive strength and one for maximal strength. For explosive strength, do six sets of three reps with about 40 percent. Forty percent of a 500-pound bench press equals 200 pounds.

It is recommended to add bands for Accommodating Resistance (AC). The advantage of the bands is that they should provide about an additional 40 percent at the top. A second advantage is that by providing over speed eccentrics the bands are used to correct the relationship of the force posture curve. Without band tensions added to the lockout, the force would be minimal.

You must understand the relationship between force and velocity. Maximum force (F_{mm}) is attained when velocity is small, but inversely, maximum velocity (V_{mm}) is attained

THROWER'S GUIDE TO STRENGTH TRAINING

when external resistance is close to zero. This should explain why AC must be added to the barbell. Read *Science and Practice of Strength Training*, pages 29 and 40, and also *Supertraining*, page 409.

The bench press should be done ballistically by lowering the weight as fast as possible, stopping it one to two inches off the chest, and reversing the barbell as fast as possible concentrically. Seventy-two hours later during the season, bench press off pieces of rubber or foam pads. This method of pressing came from the former East German training system. Westside has used this very program since the early 1980s and has produced 10 600-pound raw bench pressers plus a 700-pound raw bench.

Four sets of dumbbell presses are done every other day with a weight you can start with and you should do a set of 15 reps on each set very easily. You should change the angle each workout.

The last special exercises are the push press from behind the head. This is a good indicator of your shot put progress. Westside uses many workouts with AC. Even the very strong will use mini or monster mini bands. Push jerk or press behind the head by taking the bar or squat racks off the power rack pins.

During the season, the bench presses with pads on the chest and the push presses or jerks behind the head are very important for your success. No need to push up the squat during the season, but rather concentrate on using the Dynamic Effort Method. The Dynamic Effort Method is not used for increasing maximal strength, but only to improve the rate of force development and explosive strength. Along with jumping, this is exercise specificity for the thrower.

Everything concerning the shot putt during the season must be dynamic. During the off season the M-E Effort is best for increasing intramuscular and intermuscular coordination. Remember, the muscles and central nervous system adapt only to the load placed on them.

A major misconception in the throwing world is the idea that when your strength increases your velocity slows. This is corrected in the Westside System by using the Dynamic Effort Method 72 hours apart. Using the three-week wave with the correct percents will increase maximal strength while maintaining top velocity. For example, an 800-pound squatter will move 60 percent or 480 pounds at the same speed that a 400-pound squatter moves 60 percent or 240 pounds. To review, see the Periodization Chapter.

If you want to improve your throwing, you must train all aspects of throwing by correcting the rotation of special exercise including developing your jumping ability in a yearly training cycle. **Everything can be trained together all year long**. The weight training will provide you with the ability to become stronger and faster during the season along with maintaining strong muscles that are responsible for improving technique. And just as important, you must do some general throwing to maintain your timing and basic technique. Do not detrain by stopping some part of your training. Instead, develop a yearly plan that constantly improves movement coordination.

Chapter 8
Methods of Strength Training
Part 1-Maximal Effort Method

The thrower must be as strong as possible to throw record distances. The squats, pulls, pressing and jerks must improve as well as speed and explosive power. The best way to accomplish this is the Max Effort (M-E) method. M-E is lifting a maximum load against maximal resistance.

The M-E method is used in the training of high-class athletes in speed-strength sports. It places demands on the Central Nervous System coordination that leads to an improvement in strength. The larger the weight lifted, the more muscles are activated, and the more motor units are mobilized. The M-E method must be trained concurrently with the Dynamic Method.

To maximize speed strength, the Repeated Effort Method must also be trained to increase muscle mass around the joints. This is covered in the Periodization Chapter. While training the M-E Method, try not to get too psyched up, as it can lead to emotional fatigue. There should be one M-E workout for the upper body and one workout for the lower body with a 72-hour rest between an M-E workout and a speed-strength day.

Small workouts can be done every 12 or 24 hours. These workouts should be planned around a weakness. This can be a muscle group or correcting technique or raising General Physical Preparedness (GPP). The barbell volume will be low compared to the Dynamic Method workout. The rest intervals depend on your level of fitness. Because of sebum testosterone levels dropping in 45 minutes, the rest between sets, start fast and slow up as the weight nears your maximum. Westside's world record holders would carry a set of two and one-half pound plates to add on the last set—they called it the plan.

While Westside is not open to the public, the entire gym breaks their M-E records close to 95 percent of the time. The larger the thrower, the longer the rest intervals should be when doing M-E workouts. The barbell exercise must be rotated each week. If one uses the same barbell exercise for three weeks with a load of 90 percent or more, you will detrain due to the Law of Accommodation. This can be a loss of coordination and motivation. Remember; do not psych up often during training as this leaves little to gain at contest.

How to Conduct an M-E Workout

Strength is measured in the time to complete the lift, or the rate of velocity. M-E will be trained in slow velocity to build slow strength. Pick a special exercise that requires a very high load. For example, a lockout pin press for the bench. It is a partial movement with possibly 600 pounds.

For the next M-E workout you may choose a cambered bench bar with a five-inch deficit that only allows you to press 515 pounds. Both are maxes, but with much different amounts of weight.

Do not use a series of special exercises that require approximately the same load. Even though you have changed the special exercise, it takes close to the same time to complete the lift, which will lead to accommodation due to straining for the same amount of time. This happens in running when running the same times over and over again—the so-called speed barrier.

M-E workouts can be listed as eccentric, concentric, or isometric. When using an isometrics workout, first use dynamic exercises. (Caution: only hold your breath for two or three seconds for respiratory system health.) Only 10 percent of training should be done with isometrics.

The Westside M-E system is based on doing only all-time records, just like the Russians. The Bulgarians would count M-E attempts on a daily max, not an all-time record. Doing dynamic exercises does not differ from isometric effort.

It does no good to be strong in the wrong exercises. Neuromuscular changes are different in different special exercises, so choose them carefully.

M-E calls for doing a one rep max. When doing two or three reps per set you'll build strength endurance as you find yourself conserving your strength to complete the second or third rep.

Caution: It requires high energy to break M-E records. Remember to switch special exercises each week to avoid accommodation. You should check for high blood pressure at rest. Look also for depression or fatigue or having anxiety. None of this will happen when using the Westside M-E System as long as you switch each week and use the three-week pendulum wave periodization that is explained in the seventy-five-page Periodization Chapter.

You are a thrower, so train for throwing. Box squats, pulls, presses and jerks must be your main concern. This is the Principle of Specificity. You must pick about six special exercises to rotate for upper body and lower body. Roughly 100 M-E workouts are shown in the Periodization Chapter from which to choose. You will soon find the ones that work best for your body. Do not do what does not work for you. It is that simple.

Leg and Back Exercises

1. Rack Pull
2. Box Pull
3. Sumo and Close Stance
4. Low Box Squat
5. High Box Squat
6. Power Clean
7. Power Snatch

Use wide stance and close stance for squat and pulls.

Upper Body

8. Pin Press
9. Push Press Behind Head
10. Bench with Pad or Boards on Chest

THROWER'S GUIDE TO STRENGTH TRAINING

11. Floor Press

12. Incline Press

13. All Pressing with Rubber Bands

14. Dumbbells Presses all Four Angles

Use close and wide grips.

This is just a sample to rotate each week. For more, look at the Periodization Chapter.

Chapter 8
Methods of Strength Training
Part 2-Dynamic Method

The Importance of Speed-Strength

Many throwers concern themselves with maximal strength. In many discussions about weight training for throwers, the talk turns to comparing how strong their lifts are compared to how far they throw. The maximal strength of a thrower is, of course, very important, but maximal strength comes second to maximal speed.

While reading *Science and Practice of Strength Training* (p. 116), I found a passage where V. M. Zatsiorsky talks about a shot putter who has a 550-pound bench press then increases to 661 pounds with no gain in the shot putt. We know that M-E training is not recommended for improving the rate of force development in top athletes. To build explosive strength, the Dynamic Method must be trained in the same week 72 hours after your M-E day. It is impossible to attain Fmm in fast movements when training with intermediate resistance. Use

THROWER'S GUIDE TO STRENGTH TRAINING

the M-E workout for building maximal strength and the Dynamic Method for improving force development.

A test for a thrower would be to compare his or her top throw with how fast he or she moved weights in the range of 75 percent to 85 percent.

Throwing is a Dynamic Effort Training Method. During the competitive season the thrower should concentrate on maintaining a high level squat—let's say 700 pounds. There is no need to push the squat, but instead, perform the push jerk behind the head and the bench press with foam pads on the chest.

To maintain the 700-pound squat, train with the program below using 50 to 60 percent plus 25 percent band tension:

1. Week 1—350 pounds x 6x3 reps plus 25 percent band tension
2. Week 2—385 pounds x 6x3 reps plus 25 percent band tension
3. Week 3—420 pounds x 6x3 reps plus 25 percent band tension
4. Week 4—350 pounds x 6x3 reps plus 25 percent band tension

The bar speed must be approximately .8 or .9/ms. On the fourth week, you go back to 50 percent and repeat. If possible switch bars that you are using to squat.

According to the data compiled by A. D. Ermakov and N. S. Atanasov in their research with 780 highly skilled lifters, the weights lifted while training for speed strength is 75 percent to 85 percent used at 50 percent of the training. This information can be found in *Managing the Training of Weightlifters* (1982) by N. P. Laputin and V. G. Oleshko.

Why not lift a 700-pound squat for zero reps? Like when throwing shots of different weights, the throwing distance and initial velocity of the shot increases as the shot weight decreases. By using sub maximal weight in the Dynamic Effort Method, the motion velocity stays high—at least .8/ms. Plus, by doing 6x3 reps or 18 optimal lifts, you are doing 18 maximal exertions. This method also teaches explosive strength or the ability to exert maximal forces in minimal time.

Because the weights are sub maximal, rubber bands must account for 25 percent of the load according to the research of the author for the current data of 92 male lifters who officially squat 800 pounds to 1,250 pounds.

If you look at the posture strength curves as the barbell begins to decelerate at the final stages of a lift in multi-joint movements, the ability to apply maximal force is impossible. The bands attached to the bar provide Accommodating Resistance (AC). This provides maximal tension throughout the complete range of motion. In *Supertraining*, Dr. Siff explains Compensatory Acceleration Training, or CAT. The CAT method provides the athlete to increase muscle tension by trying to move the load as fast as possible. Dr. Fred Hatfield said, "No one can lift a heavy weight slow." But with less than maximal loads, this is impossible, too, due to the force-posture relationship and the human strength curve.

After the speed-strength squats, box jumps are done. To work on improving explosive strength, do 40 jumps two times a week. Box jumping is a very predictable test of your explosive strength.

As a testament to the program, Rob Golabek came to Westside after not making any gains in not only the shot, but also his weight training. His squatting was plateaued at 600 pounds. After four and one-half months of specialized training, his top squat was 900 pounds. He used the Westside System with an M-E day on Monday for his squats and pulls, and Friday was his Dynamic Method day for squats and pulls. The first three-week pendulum wave was set for a 600-pound squat.

There are two important things Rob did to start the program. First, it was based on his actual squat record. Second, Rob's coach had never used speed-strength training for squatting. But instead, he had used the outdated Western Periodization based on a new hypothetical goal. This seldom works for a mathematical reason—you cannot base the percentages on a squat you cannot achieve. Rob worked up to a max after doing two three-week waves. Speed pull deadlifts were done after squats using a snatch grip to build the traps. Lots of reverse hypers, four times a week inverse curls, and very heavy belt squatting along with lots of static holds for the glutes and hips were part of the program. Rotational work in the A.T.P. Belt Squat Machine™ was included, plus, jumping 40 jumps two times a week. This is no secret, but rather a system that combines building maximal strength along with training for explosive strength by pumping and barbell training with weights ranging from 30 percent to 40 percent while at the same time working on speed strength ranging from 75 percent to 85 percent by using the Combination of Resistance Methods for which the author is known worldwide.

Rob did not throw for 16 months, but increased his throw from 19.74 meters to 20 meters. In the 16 months Rob worked on his technique with a new coach. He then started training throwers to increase their technique along with continuing to use the Westside System.

Some special exercises Rob used were incline dumbbells presses every other day. He changed the angle on the incline one notch each workout. He worked his triceps very hard and constantly pushed up the box jump record; no throws for 16 months, but constantly working on technique and improving on the three velocities. This meant improving his M-E training along with speed strength training and improving his jumping ability on the boxes and breaking records on his long jumps.

While Westside does not suggest not throwing for 16 months, Rob did improve his best all-time record. But it shows how important speed strength training is to throwing. You must learn to train all aspects of training all year long by working on all three velocities along with perfecting your technique.

Most important, you must discard block periodization and implement the three-week wave system of training—the Westside System.

Chapter 8
Methods of Strength Training
Part 3-Repeated Effort Method

Westside uses the Repeated Effort Method almost exclusively for single-joint training. This means all extension work for the knee, hip, back, elbow and neck. You must train all types of muscle fiber. Fast twitch tires first, so you must train close to failure to train all possible muscle units (MU). High reps are necessary to cause the muscles to be fatigued. If they are not fatigued, they are not trained. Training will produce muscle hypertrophy.

All athletes will not fatigue at the same rate. Power athletes like weightlifters, powerlifters, or sprinters will tire quickly due to possessing mostly fast twitch fiber—some times up to 70 percent. While endurance athletes—like long distance runners—have high amounts of slow twitch fiber, up to 70 percent slow fiber. The coach must know the different. Great throwers must have a high degree of fast twitch muscles.

Exercising has a side effect ... fatigue. If one must do high volume for single-joint training, it is advisable to stop just short of failure. This will make it possible to do several sets. This is basic muscle recruitment. Top athletes can coordinate the work in a single muscle or a muscle group. This requires a superior ability to use intra muscular and inter muscular coordination.

The higher level athlete can achieve more fast-twitch motor units. Lesser skilled athletes do not have the ability to recruit as many fast-twitch motor units as their highly skilled training partners. The size principle theory of training can explain it in more detail.

This brings us to inter muscular coordination. After a multi-joint movement—like the five classical lifts and including any multi-joint special exercises like a Goodmorning or a high pull—you must concentrate on single-joint isolated movements. The single-joint movements will compliment the multi-joint exercises and improve muscle imbalances that cause injuries.

When training for eccentric strength, concentric strength, or static strength, always end the workout with the Repeated Effort Method Training on a single muscle or a single muscle group to near failure.

Do not do ultra high reps in the classical lifts because the weakest muscle group will fail and an injury will occur. Certainly you have seen it when someone does very high reps in the squat or deadlift and hurt their lower back or pulled a hamstring. It is common in bench pressing to hurt a pec or shoulder. Then, it becomes reoccurring. This is why you must rain a muscle group that is lagging behind other muscle groups.

Caution: We are not talking about body building. A body builder will try to enlarge the muscle between joints to make it appear to have larger muscles. On the other hand, a man or woman who wants to be strong must strengthen the muscles around the joints.

THROWER'S GUIDE TO STRENGTH TRAINING

When training for absolute strength, you must do several sets to near failure. Three sets of 10 reps will not work with this program. The triceps need from "go" to roughly 100 total reps in one workout. For example, the author would do eight sets of eight reps with 30 seconds rest in the dumbbell roll-backs with 70-pound dumbbells. After doing ___ straight bar extensions after his bench set. This was followed by 200 reps in the triceps push down with rubber bands to strength the connective tissue. The goal is to build large muscles while at the same time increasing coordination of muscle activity by the CNS.

Westside only has advanced lifters and other athletes. To become an advanced athlete, you must train four large workouts a week plus at least four small— meaning 20 to 40 minutes— non-stop workouts with small special exercises. This is for strength building and GPP, which is closely related to SPP.

The Westside System calls for high volume. The training is divided 20 percent with the barbell and 80 percent with small special exercises. Do the largest barbell special exercises first and the small special exercises last on the four large workout days. For the short, small workouts only do small special exercises, sometimes super setting like a body builder, except they are to build strength. This means extensions for the arms, knees, back and neck. Also do raises for the delts or leg raises. Pull sleds for upper and lower back as well as for abs. Choose well as it does no good to be strong in the wrong exercises. A special note: one of Westside's top lifters would do 1,000 crunches and lat pull-downs. I asked him what he received from all the lat pull-downs. His reply? "Nothing. I just like to do them." Case closed.

Special work on a Reverse Hyper™ and in the A.T.P. Belt Squat Machine™ constitutes a large portion of our volume for legs, hips, and lower back. Exercise must be grouped together and in the right sequence. This is very important to the success of your training for any and all sports training.

Remember, without a plan, you plan to fail.

Chapter 9
Combining Weight Training and Throws

Westside Barbell's weight training programming for throwers is well documented from the early 1980s with Kevin Akins and his 70-foot 10-inch shot put. Kevin trained at Westside and his training was set forth for optimal gains in strength and power along with recovery to prevent fatigue and soreness and, most important, meet preparation.

While doing an internship at Westside Barbell, coach Rob Golabek was kind enough to outline from his own experiences several workouts to guide you that combine all phases of training the thrower.

Lifting and Throwing

By Rob Golabek

As a coach, my job is to give my athletes every possible opportunity to become the best athlete they can be. I believe this is achieved through proper event coaching, a structured strength and conditioning program, and constant communication between any and all coaches involved. Being a former division one student-athlete and professional thrower, I have a solid understanding of what it takes to truly develop an athlete and maximize his or her skill set. Every athlete possesses the potential to be great; they just need the right tools and support to make it happen.

Figure 1.0 - Standing Throw Positions

THROWER'S GUIDE TO STRENGTH TRAINING

Figure 1.1 - Half Throw

Figure 1.2 - Entry Work

A true understanding of what it takes to become the best possible athlete is something I believe can only be developed from years of personal experience and constant improvement of the coach's personal skill set. With any athlete I work with, my first order of business is to determine the individual's strengths and weaknesses. By identifying an athlete's weaknesses, we are able to spend more time on those particular areas that need improvement and I can help streamline the learning process. My training philosophy is based on efficiency and the faster that the areas of weakness are determined, the faster they can be worked on, improved, and transformed into strengths.

Implementation of wave periodization allows athletes to achieve consistent in-season results through hard work, while allowing for optimal performances at major competitions. My programs are designed to focus heavily on eliminating any weaknesses (as determined from my training assessment) while simultaneously enhancing overall performance. Below is an example of what a normal week of strength training would look like for my athletes.

Monday:

Max Effort Lower Day
- Start with any variation of squats, deadlifts, Goodmornings, cleans, etc.
- I like to vary bars, depths, stance, and/or resistance to constantly challenge the athlete and eliminate accommodation. This also gives the athlete something to look forward to and helps motivate him/her to achieve personal records, which sets up the athlete to crave success based on personal performances.
- After the main movement comes a series of auxiliary lifts that build general physical preparedness and addresses the athlete's weak points. This holds true for the rest of the week's training sessions.

Tuesday:

Recovery Day

- Use this day as a "recovery day" in order to give the athlete time to recover between heavy workouts and address problem areas.
- This will include, but is not limited to, foam rolling, mobility work, additional abdominal training, plyometrics, and medicine ball drills.

Figure 1.3 - Med Ball Slam

Figure 1.4 - Med Ball Vertical Throw

Figure 1.5 - Med Ball Overhead Throw

Wednesday:

Max Effort Upper Day

- Wednesdays are our max effort upper day; 72 hours after our last maximum effort day.
- Similar to our heavy lower body day; constantly changing bars, grips, degree of incline, boards, resistance, etc. gives the athlete variation, which keeps training both effective and enjoyable.

Thursday:

Recovery Day

- This is another recovery day similar to Tuesday's training routine.
- During the preseason this will be used as a cardio day. Given the group of athletes, the mileage will be minimal, but the underlying fitness requirements will remain the same.
- Some things I've found beneficial are stadiums, weighted sled drags, pool workouts, and "fun cardio."
- Fun cardio is where the athletes pick what they want to do. Activities range from flag football to freeze tag and consist of any exercise to elevate heart rate and increase work capacity.

Friday:

Dynamic Effort Lower

- Friday is our dynamic lower day. In order to become a great thrower, you have to be strong AND explosive.
- Utilizing the dynamic effort allows the athlete to train based off percentages dictated by their current strength levels, not estimates.
- This eliminates the possibility for overtraining and takes the guesswork out of the athlete's hands.

- Utilizing bands and chains for accommodated resistance will allow for substantial gains in speed strength and strength speed.

Saturday:

Dynamic Effort Upper

- Similar to our dynamic lower day; the athletes will utilize a sub-maximal weight with maximum effort for specific sets and reps with calculated rest periods.
- This allows strength to be developed without overexerting the central nervous system and raising the athletes GPP.

The athlete's workouts are designed to be very efficient in the sense that we work primarily on bringing up the individual's weak points while addressing overall strength development. Each strength training session is roughly an hour in length, not including a dynamic warm-up and mobility drills and is finished after a stretching routine and cool down.

While strength training is an integral part of being a successful throws coach, nothing is more important than the technical progression of an athlete. Having worked with some of the best throws coaches in the world, I've learned how to develop athletes ranging from beginning throwers who have never thrown, all the way to working with Olympic athletes. Although the margin for error differs with experience level, the fundamental concepts remain the same. This is an extremely important part of my training philosophy: the actual development of the athlete.

Teaching them how to perfect the simple things allows for consistency in performances.

Below is a general outline on how I implement progression in the throwing events. This example is designed for peaking at the conference championships and it can be adjusted for the postseason schedule at any time. Starting with the most important meets on the schedule and working backward, I develop a training program geared for big throws at the end of the year. Tapering my athletes off the weights and changing the weight of training implements develops competition timing and ensures the best chance for great performances.

October—November:

- This period of time will be used to develop a relationship with the athletes while indirectly evaluating their current training state.
- This is followed by discussing the importance of goal setting.
- I have each athlete write out personal goals then hold individual meetings to address how we can achieve them together.
- Then I introduce very basic drills including PVC pipe drills, medicine ball drills, visualization work, footwork drills and a variety of other movements to help develop proper motor pathways for the throwing events.
- This is all without actually releasing the implements. This puts the focus on the movement, not the distance.
- Along with developing a solid foundation of the throw it allows us to do hundreds of drills per week without the physical abuse of throwing.

Figure 1.6 - Med Ball Standing Throw

Figure 1.7 - Med Ball Step-to-Throw

Figure 1.8 - Med Ball Half Throw

Figure 1.9 - Med Ball Finger Flicks

Figure 2.0 - Med Ball Entry Work

November—December: (Leading up to the first meet):

- During this phase of the season we begin to bring the implements into training.
- We start every day with a series of drills relating to the day's practice to help set the mind up for the event. The closer we get to the first meet, the emphasis shifts to developing a game plan for the competition.
- What our goals are, how will we approach the competition, what coaching cues worked best during that week of training and how we deal with the unexpected events that always seem to come up during track meets.

December—February/Early March:

- At this point in the season we have fallen into a routine and are working out issues and making progress towards technical mastery of the throw.
- We are putting in a good deal of volume in the circle and the weight room.
- When we hit late January through early February, we are beginning the three-week taper from weight training, allowing the athletes to feel very fresh and explosive.
- Decreasing the volume of throws ensures athletes are feeling fresh and ready to compete.
- Drills become much more precise and our film review sessions are more geared to small cues opposed to large technical flaws.

March—Late April:

- After a few days off from throwing, we are right back to work in the circle.
- With the transition to the outdoor season, we have new events to learn and new drills to master.

Late April—End of May:

- This period is very similar to the indoor championship season.
- The foundation has been set; now it's about refining the movement and building confidence with consistency.
- Doing the little things perfectly over and over during the entire season allows for confidence in pressure situations.
- This along with backing off in the weight room gives the athlete the best possible opportunity for big performances.

Off Season Training:

- During this time, the athlete has time to reflect on the previous season and develop a game plan for the next year.
- We look at our goals from the beginning of the season and see how we did overall and how we can improve.
- We begin our summer lifting program based on the prior year's progress by addressing weaknesses that I believe will allow for an even more successful upcoming season.

Below is an example of a standard three-week wave of training. The sets and reps are on the higher end to help build a base for the athletes. This is also known as GPP (general physical preparedness) or work capacity.

The Framework

WEEK 1-

Monday:

Warm Up: Banded TKE / Banded Ankle Mobility / Dumbbell RDL / Banded Good Mornings

1- Close Stance Low Box Squat vs. Mini Bands 1 Rep Max
2- Conventional Stiff Leg Sumo RDL 4x15
3- Med Ball Russian Twist x 100
4- Leg Press 3x15
5- Wide Grip Seated Row 5x15
6- Banded Hamstring Curls x125

Louie Simmons

Foam Roll & Stretch 10 Minute Minimum

Tuesday:

Box Jumps with weight 5x5 / Sled Drags 6x 60 yards / Abs / Foam Roll & Stretch 10 Minute Minimum

Wednesday:

Warm Up: Dumbbell Incline Bench 4x25 / Y + T Raise 2x15 / Banded Face Pulls

1- First Click Incline 1 Rep Max
2- Wide Grip reps 3x8-10
3- Wide Grip Lat Pull down 4x15
4- Machine Abs x 100
5- Mini Band Pull Apart 3x25 / Rope Triceps 4x25
6- Y+ Ts 50 each / Dumbbell Hammer Curls 100 total

Foam Roll & Stretch 10 Minute Minimum

Thursday:

Box Jumps with weight 5x5 / Sled Drags 6x60 yards / Abs / Foam Roll & Stretch 10 Minute Minimum

Friday:

Warm up: TKE / TKF / Banded Ankle Mobility 3x30 each leg / Sumo RDL 2x15 / Body Weight Wide Stance Squats 4x10

1- Wide Stance Box Squat 10x2 with 45 percent VS 25 percent band tension

*Rest time 50-55 seconds max

2- Sumo Speed Pull VS Mini Bands w/ 50 percent 5x5

*Same rest protocol

3- Barbell Clean and Press 3x10 Fast

4- Dumbbell Obliques 100

5- Back Hypers with weight 5x15 / Banded hammy curls 4x50

6- Groiners / Clamshells 5x15 each

Foam Roll & Stretch 10 Minute Minimum

Saturday:

Warm Up: Y + T raise 2x25 / Dumbbell Bench 4x 25 / Face Pulls 3x15

1- Close Grip Speed Bench 9x3 with 40% vs. Mini Bands

2- Cable Face Pulls 5x15

3- Barbell Hang Clean and Press 5x15

*45 second rest between sets

4- Crunches w/w 100 total

5- Mini Band Pull apart 100 total

6- Curls / Tricep rope pushdowns 4x25 (superset these)

Foam Roll & Stretch 10 Minute Minimum

WEEK 2

Monday:

Warm Up: Banded TKE / Banded Ankle Mobility / Dumbbell RDL / Banded Good Mornings

1- Sumo Pulls vs. Mini Bands 1 Rep Max

2- Deficit Dumbbell RDL 4x15

3- Cable Abs x 100

4- Banded Goodmornings 3x15

5- Wide Grip Seated Row 5x15

6- Banded Hamstring Curls x 125

Foam Roll & Stretch 10 Minute Minimum

Tuesday:

Box Jumps with weight 5x5 / Sled Drags 6x60 yards / Abs / Foam Roll & Stretch 10 Minute Minimum

Wednesday:

Warm Up: Dumbbell Incline Bench 4x25 / Y + T Raise 2x15 / Banded Face Pulls

1- Floor Press 1 Rep Max

2- Wide Grip reps 3x8-10

3- Barbell High Pulls 4x15

4- Machine Abs x 100

5- Mini Band Pull Apart 3x25 / DB Triceps 4x25

6- Y+ Ts 50 each / Dumbbell Hammer Curls 100 total

Foam Roll & Stretch 10 Minute Minimum

Thursday:

Box Jumps with weight 5x5 / Sled Drags 6x 60 yards / Abs / Foam Roll & Stretch 10 Minute Minimum

Friday:

Warm up: TKE / TKF / Banded Ankle Mobility 3x30 each leg / Sumo RDL 2x15 / Body Weight Wide Stance Squats 4x10

1- Wide Stance Box Squat 8x2 with 50% VS 25% band tension

*Rest time 50-55 seconds max

2- Sumo Speed VS Mini Bands Pull w/ 50% 5x5

*Same rest protocol

3- Barbell Clean and Press 3x10 Fast

4- Dumbbell Obliques 100 total

5- Back Hypers with weight 5x15 / Banded hammy curls 4x50

6- Groiners / Clamshells 5x15 each

Foam Roll & Stretch 10 Minute Minimum

Saturday:

Warm Up: Y + T raise 2x25 / DB Bench 4x 25 / Face Pulls 3x15

1- Neutral Grip Speed Bench 9x3 with 40% vs. Min Bands

2- Banded Lat Pull-down 5x15

3- Barbell Hang Clean and Press 5x15

*45 second rest between sets

4- Crunches w/w 100 total

5- Mini Band Pull apart 100 total

6- Curls / Tricep rope pushdowns 4x25 (super set these)

Foam Roll & Stretch 10 Minute Minimum

WEEK 3

Monday:

Warm Up: Banded TKE / Banded Ankle Mobility / Dumbbell RDL / Banded Good Mornings

1- Front Box Squat vs. Chains 1 Rep Max

2- Sumo RDL 4x15

3- Cable Abs x 100

4- Banded Goodmornings 3x15

5- Snatch Grip Shrugs 5x15

6- Banded Hamstring Curls x 125

Foam Roll & Stretch 10 Minute Minimum

Tuesday:

Box Jumps with weight 5x5 / Sled Drags 6x 60 yards / Abs / Foam Roll & Stretch 10 Minute Minimum

Wednesday:

Warm Up: Dumbbell Incline Bench 4x25 / Y + T Raise 2x15 / Banded Face Pulls

1- Football Bar Bench 1 Rep Max

2- Close Grip reps 3x8-10

3- Snatch Pulls 3x8

4- Banded Abs x 100

5- Mini Band Pull Apart 3x25 // DB Triceps 4x25

6- Y+ Ts 50 each // Dumbbell Hammer Curls 100 total

Foam Roll & Stretch 10 Minute Minimum

Thursday:

Box Jumps with weight 5x5 / Sled Drags 6x 60 yards / Abs / Foam Roll & Stretch 10 Minute Minimum

Friday:

Warm up: TKE / TKF / Banded Ankle Mobility 3x30 each leg / Sumo RDL 2x15 / Body Weight Wide Stance Squats 4x10

THROWER'S GUIDE TO STRENGTH TRAINING

1- Wide Stance Box Squat 6x2 with 55% vs. 25% band tension

*Rest time 50-55 seconds max

2- Sumo Speed vs. Mini Bands Pull with 50% 5x5

*Same rest protocol

3- Dumbbell Clean and Press 3x10 Fast

4- Plate Twists x 100

5- Back Hypers with weight 5x15 / Banded hammy curls 4x50

6- Groiners / Clamshells 5x15 each

Foam Roll & Stretch 10 Minute Minimum

Saturday:

Warm Up: Y + T raise 2x25 / DB Bench 4x 25 / Face Pulls 3x15

1- Wide Grip Speed Bench 9x3 with 40% vs. Min Bands

2- V Bar Pull-down 5x15

3- Barbell Push Press 5x15

*45 second rest between sets

4- Crunches w/w 100 total

5- Mini Band Pull apart 100 total

6- Curls / Tricep rope pushdowns 4x25 (super set these)

Foam Roll & Stretch 10 Minute Minimum

 This is just a small glimpse into what can be done with conjugate programming. You can switch in any max effort variation you like, just make adaptations for resistance. If you want to max power cleans, jerk press, snatch, front squat, push press or any other lift / variation. The only limiting factor is your creativity.

 Another important topic I feel that needs to be brought up is proper equipment in the weight room. All sports have some protective equipment. Pads, special shoes, gloves, eye protection or whatever else you can think up. Why not in the weight room? You expect athletes to move thousands of pounds of weight on a daily basis with just the clothes on their back? To me that is unacceptable. Athletes should be wearing knee/ elbow sleeves, wrist wraps, belts, and most importantly squatting briefs. Keeping an athlete healthy and in proper positions seems like a pretty good idea to me and why it isn't utilized more is beyond me. I'm not saying a golfer needs to be in a full canvas suit, but I firmly believe they would benefit from a good par of power pants to save their back and hips from training.

One of the most important concepts of sports specific conjugate training is general physical preparedness. You must be in shape at all times. As an athlete you have the predictability of 1 knowing when and where your competitions are going to take place, so it's imperative to prepare for them to the best of your ability. There are some situations that you can't foresee, so you need to be able to adapt and rely on your training.

A perfect example of this is my personal experience in the shot put. In 2013 I competed at the USA indoor national championship in Albuquerque, New Mexico, where I threw just over 19 meters. After that meet I began coaching at the division 1, and as any coach will tell you this is a very demanding job. I spent six hours a day coaching my throwers in all events. This included, but isn't limited to, event specific drills, video analysis, visualization, and body mechanic analysis. At no time during this period of time did I throw any implements in the competitive sense or partake in any track meets. All drilling was on a coach to athlete technical basis. In 2016 the team I was coaching had a tune up meet before the conference championship. The meet was very small, so I decided to dust off the shoes and compete to help bring up the energy for the meet. In the competition I ended up throwing 19.96 M qualifying for 2016 Olympic Trials.

THROWER'S GUIDE TO STRENGTH TRAINING

As surprised as I was at the result, I understood why it happened. For three years all I did was lift weights in a conjugate-based program and drill for my event. I already knew how to compete, so it was a perfect combination. My point here is not to brag, but to express the importance of conjugate training and technical development.

About Rob Golabek

Rob Golabek is a Westside Barbell certified special strengths coach and contributing researcher for Westside. In 2013 Rob earned his key and a training spot with the morning crew and has maintained a positive relationship and working for Louie ever since. Under the guidance of Louie Simmons, Rob qualified for the 2012 and 2016 Olympic trials in shot put. Rob has utilized the Westside training philosophies with all his athletes ranging from youth sports to a host of professional athletes. In college Rob was a 4x Division One All-American and multiple time conference champion for Jim Garnham Sr. at The University at Buffalo.

References and Selected Bibliography

Blackburn, J. Troy, and Marc F. Norcross. "The effects of isometric and isotonic training on hamstring stiffness and anterior cruciate ligament loading mechanisms." *Journal of Electromyography and Kinesiology*. 24. 1. 2014: 98-103.

Bondarchuk, Anatoliv. *Champion School, A Year to Year Model to Developing Elite* Athletes. Michigan: Ultimate Athlete Concepts. 2015.

Bondarchuk, Anatoliv. *Transfer of Training in Sports*. Michigan: Ultimate Athlete Concepts. 2007.

Bondarchuk, Anatoliv. *Transfer of Training in Sports II*. Michigan: Ultimate Athlete Concepts. 2010.

Bondarchuk, Anatoliv. *Transfer of Training in Sports III*. Michigan: Ultimate Athlete Concepts. 2017.

Carr, Gerald A. *Fundamentals of Track and Field, 2nd Edition*. Champaign, IL: Human Kinetics. 1999.

Fraley, Bob and Jacoby, Ed. *Complete Book of Jumps*. Champaign, IL: Human Kinetics. 1995.

Issurin, Vladimir. *Building the Modern Athlete, Scientific Advancements & Training Innovations*. Michigan: Ultimate Athlete Concepts. 2015.

Kenney, W. Larry, Jack Wilmore, and David Costill. *Physiology of Sport and Exercise 6th Edition*. Champaign, IL: Human Kinetics. 2015.

Komi, P.V. *Strength and Power in Sport*. Great Britain: Blackwell Science Ltd. 1992.

Kubo, Keitaro, Tomonobu Ishigaki, and Toshihiro Ikebukuro. "Effects of Plyometric and Isometric Training on Muscle and Tendon Stiffness in Vivo." *Physiological Reports* 5.15 (3017): e13374. PMC Web. 16 Nov. 2017.

Kurz, Thomas. *Science of Sports Training*. Island Pond, VT: Stadon Publishing Company, Inc. 1990.

Laputin, N. P. and V. G. Oleshko. *Fundamentals of Special Strength-Training in Sport*. 1982.

Laputin, N.P. and Oleshko, V.G. (1982). *Managing the Training of Weightlifters*. (A. Charniga, Trans.) Livonia, MI: Sportivny Press. (Original work published in 1982, Kiev, Russia: Zdorov'ya Publishers.)

Lasocki, Andzej. *The World Atlas of Exercises for Track and Field*. Sportpress, 2001.

Rogers, Joseph L. USA *Track & Field*. Coaching Manual. Champaign, IL. 2005

Schmolinsky, G. *Track and Field*. Berlin, Germany: Sportverlag. 1982.

Siff, Mel. C. *Supertraining*. Denver: Supertraining Institute, 2003.

Simmons, Louie. *Bench Press Manual*. Columbus, OH: Westside4Athletes, 2009.

Simmons, Louie. *Explosive Strength Development for Jumping*. Columbus, OH: Westside4Athletes, 2014.

Simmons, Louie. *Olympic Weightlifting Strength Manual*. Columbus, OH: Westside4Athletes, 2016.

Simmons, Louie. *Special Strength Development for All Sports*. Columbus, OH: Westside4Athletes, 2015.

Simmons, Louie. *Squat and Deadlift Manual*. Columbus, OH: Westside4Athletes, 2011.

Simmons, Louie. *Strength Manual for Running*. Columbus, OH: Westside4Athletes, 2017.

Simmons, Louie. *Westside Barbell Book of Methods*. Columbus, OH: Westside4Athletes, 2007.

Starzynski, Tadeusz and Henryk Sozansky. *Explosive Power and Jumping Ability for All Sports*. Island Pond, VT: Stadion Publishing Company, 1995.

Svantesson, U., et al. "Comparison of muscle and tendon stiffness, jumping ability muscle strength and fatigue in the plantar flexors." *Scandinavian journal of medicine and science in sports* 8.5 (1998): 252-256.

USA Track & Field. *Track & Field Coaching Essentials*. USATF Properties, LLC. 2015.

Verkhoshansky, Yuri, and Natalia Verkhoshansky. *Special Strength Training: Manual for Coaches*. Rome: Verkhoshansky Sstm, 2011.

Verkhoshansky, Yuri. *Managing the Training of Weightlifting*. Sportivny Press, 1982.

Verkhoshansky, Yuri and Natalia Verkhoshansky, *Special Strength Training Manual for Coaches*. Verkhoshansky.com, 2011.

Yessis, M. *Biomechanics and Kinesiology of Exercise*. Michigan: Ultimate Athletic Concepts. 2013.

Yessis, M. *Secrets of Soviet Sports Fitness and Training*. Michigan: Ultimate Athletic Concepts. 1987.

Zatsiorsky, V. M. and William J. Kraemer *Science and Practice of Strength Training*. Champaign, IL: Human Kinetics, 1995.